A Mother's War

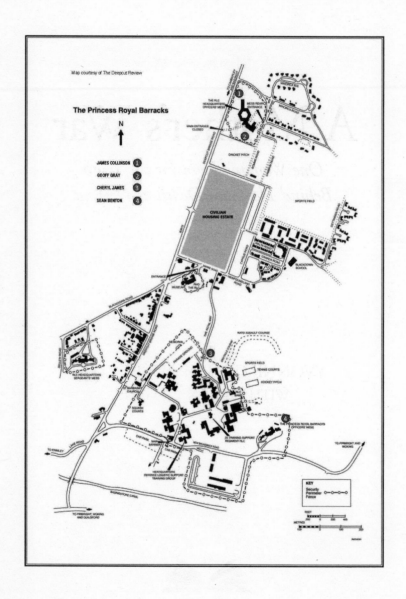

Map courtesy of The Deepcut Review

The Princess Royal Barracks

N

JAMES COLLINSON   1

GEOFF GRAY   2

CHERYL JAMES   3

SEAN BENTON   4

A Mother's War

One Woman's Fight for the Truth
Behind Her Son's Death at Deepcut

YVONNE COLLINSON HEATH
WITH DEREK LAMBIE

MAINSTREAM
PUBLISHING

EDINBURGH AND LONDON

First published in Great Britain in 2013 by

MAINSTREAM PUBLISHING COMPANY

(EDINBURGH) LTD

7 Albany Street

Edinburgh EH1 3UG

ISBN 9781780575940

This book is a work of non-fiction based on the life,
experiences and recollections of the author.

A catalogue record for this book is available
from the British Library

Printed in Great Britain by
CPI Group (UK) Ltd, Croydon, CR0 4YY

1 3 5 7 9 10 8 6 4 2

To the memory of Sean Benton, Cheryl James,
Geoff Gray and James Collinson.

Forever in our hearts.

Contents

Contents

Preface

I will never forget the phone call that changed my life for ever. It was shortly after 8 a.m. on a crisp spring morning: the kind of morning that makes you feel glad to be alive. Outside, the birds were chirping and the sunshine was streaming in through the window. The phone had been ringing for a while, but I chose to ignore it. It was Sunday, the day of rest, after all. It rang again. And again. And again. Little did I know, as I sauntered downstairs to find out who on earth was calling at such an ungodly hour, that my world was about to change for ever.

'It's James,' said the panicked voice of my estranged husband, referring to our eldest son, a trainee soldier with the Royal Logistic Corps. 'He's dead.'

And that was that. At 8.15 a.m. on Sunday, 24 March 2002, the life I knew came to a shuddering halt.

My name is Yvonne Heath, but I am better known under my former married name, Yvonne Collinson. You might have heard of me, but at the very least you're probably familiar with the tragic story of my son, and my 11-year-long quest for answers over his untimely death. James was just 17 when he died: barely 17, having only celebrated his birthday 15 weeks earlier. He was six weeks into his training at the Princess Royal Barracks in Surrey – a place more commonly referred to as Deepcut – when he was found dead with a single gunshot wound to the head. In the days that followed, the Army told us he had killed himself – one senior officer even heartlessly declared it was a case of 'one body, one bullet, draw your own conclusion' – but we refused to believe it. We could not accept that our son would have willingly taken a gun to his own head. He had his whole life ahead of him; he was just a boy. We continue to harbour doubts to this day.

It's fair to say that I have been on an extraordinary journey over the past decade or so, and if you had told me on 21 March 2002 that my life would pan out as it has I simply wouldn't have believed you. I have gone from an ordinary mother and care worker, living quietly in the fair city of Perth in Scotland, to someone many people now recognise in the street. I have been places I could never have imagined and appeared in more newspapers and been on more television shows than I even knew existed, having spent the best part of 11 years striving to find out what happened to my James. I have chased government ministers around the corridors of the House of Commons, protested in front of royalty and taken my fight to the very gates of Downing Street. And, standing shoulder to shoulder with the parents of three other young soldiers who also died at Deepcut, I have fronted countless media campaigns demanding a public inquiry into the place now dubbed the 'camp from hell'. Yet all of it – so far – has been in vain. I still have no idea why my son died at that barracks.

It feels like an eternity has passed since that fateful night James was found lying by the perimeter fence of the camp with part of his head blown off. I have experienced a hellish roller-coaster ride of emotions since then, that's for sure, and not a day goes by that I don't think of my son.

The deaths of the four soldiers at Deepcut – Sean Benton, Cheryl James and Geoff Gray completing the tragic quartet – have been much documented over the years, particularly in the British press. However, only part of the story has ever really been told. At the time, there was only so much the families of the soldiers who died wanted to share about what went on behind the scenes as we tried so desperately to force an inquiry into the tragedies, and into Deepcut itself. We have rarely spoken in any detail about the horrendous treatment we endured at the hands of the Army over the years, or about the private dealings we had with politicians and senior police as our high-profile campaign fell apart.

It's now time to share that very intimate and emotional story for the first time. However, in order to do that and to give some context to the woman I was during the Deepcut years, I have to chart my own personal story. Abandoned by my father when I was a baby, I was bullied at school and I was abused, on a near daily basis, by my uncle from a young age. Somehow, though, I managed to overcome the horrors of my childhood to raise three cherished children of my own, only to see my beloved eldest son taken from me on a dark March night in 2002. Some people have told me what I have gone through is remarkable. Yet I simply believe that fate has dealt me a poor hand and that I've muddled through and survived. I have had to.

It has been suggested to me many times that I should write a book about my life experiences, from the earliest days of the abuse to the present day as I continue, even now, to fight for answers about James's death. In the past I was always against the idea because I didn't want to be accused of glamorising any of the injustices thrown my way over the last four decades. Now, though, I realise how much reading about other people's lives has helped and encouraged me to move onwards and upwards. Books about the adversity suffered by others have provided inspiration and reminded me that it doesn't matter how bad things seem; there is always someone else out there experiencing more pain and hurt. I hope this book will do the same for somebody.

The very last thing I seek is sympathy. I simply feel that without knowledge of my childhood the reader will not fully understand what made me the person I am today. Indeed, putting my thoughts on paper has helped me make some kind of sense of my past. I believe that things happen for a reason, and it may be that the terrible ordeal I endured in my younger days made me a stronger adult and prepared me for the trials and tribulations that faced me as a mother. In many ways, writing this book has also helped me to exorcise the ghosts of the past, particularly the ordeal I endured at the hands of my uncle. For decades I have lived with a heavy burden of guilt over the fact I told no one what he was doing to me, and I have agonised over whether my silence caused him to carry on and do the same to a host of other children in Perth, as you will find out. We will never know, but putting down words and recording, in black and white, the vile nature of the man has helped.

This book, for the most part, deals with the loss of my son and charts my numerous attempts to push for a public inquiry into Deepcut. However it is also about James. So little has ever been written about him, other than the circumstances surrounding the fateful night at the barracks. Yet he was more than merely a statistic: he was a son, a brother, a grandson, a nephew, a cousin, a friend. He had hopes and dreams like everybody else. He laughed. He loved. He was loved by so many. He was my James. Yes, this book charts the tragedy of James's death, but it's also about his life. As much as anything else, it's the story of the little boy who overcame the odds and fulfilled his ambition to become a soldier, only to see his life cruelly cut short before he had even reached his 18th birthday. In that sense, I hope this book is a fitting tribute to him.

As I have explained, my world collapsed on that March morning and I felt pain so intense that I genuinely wished I could die. However, unable to bring myself to believe my son could have shot himself, I found a hitherto unknown inner strength and channelled my grief into a high-profile campaign to seek out the truth. In the years that followed James's death, this quest for answers became all-consuming. It took over my life and everything – and everyone – was put on hold for a decade as I attempted to take on the Establishment. Ultimately I failed, as you will discover.

All the pieces of the jigsaw that make up my life so far are set forth in the following chapters. You will, hopefully, see that I am a very different person now to the one who grew up living with her aunt and uncle in an end-terrace three-bedroom house on the outskirts of Perth. Eleven years after James's death I continue to take one day at a time, and despite all the knock-backs, I never falter from the hope that someone who knows something about the shooting will eventually come forward with the information that will end my anguish and, finally, see justice done. Not just for me, but for my son, Private James Collinson.

This is our story.

1. Abused

AYAYAYAYAYAYAYAYAYAYAYAYAYAYAYAYAYAYAYAYAYAYAYAYAYAYAYAYAYAYAYAYAY

The sexual abuse started when I was five, or so I'm told. I don't actually remember when it began, but I have no reason to doubt it. After all, I was informed by the abuser himself, the man I had once trusted most: my uncle. I only have vague recollections of something horrible first taking place at the age of about seven or eight, but I'm assured I was much younger. In the very beginning, it only happened on holiday; then it occurred once or twice a week, but it became more frequent as the years passed. By the time I was fully aware of it, it had become a daily ritual, a chore to be undertaken every night after dinner, like washing the dishes or throwing out the rubbish.

The odd thing is that as I was growing up I didn't know it was wrong or that it didn't happen to everyone else. I had been groomed for my uncle's sick pleasure from such an early age that it had become normal behaviour and I simply factored it into my day-to-day routine: school, homework, dinner, sex, television, bed.

Uncle George seemed to relish telling me about the first time he had taken advantage of me. He confessed he had an attraction to children and boasted about his sexual exploits with schoolgirls in Hong Kong during his time in the Royal Navy in the 1960s. 'I like 'em young,' he would say. I was a very early developer and was wearing a bra at six years old. By the time I was eight, I'd already had my first period. I was more mature than I should have been for my age. It made me perfect prey, it would seem.

The first time I recall my uncle doing something to me was just before I hit puberty, so I must have been about seven, maybe slightly older. Uncle George had taken me to bed and proceeded to rape me, but when he finished the condom split. I can clearly remember his state of absolute panic as he dragged me through to the bathroom and stood me up on the toilet pan before using a bath sponge to try to clean me out. He soaked the sponge in cold water and put it between my legs while squeezing it as tight as he could. He then tried to push it inside me, and I could see the horror on his face. He was frightened, I was frightened, and it was a traumatic experience. Before me was a man who normally appeared very calm and in control, but something had caused him to get into a state I hadn't seen him in before. At seven, I was too young to understand why. This is the age at which I was expecting Uncle George to say he had first taken advantage of me. Not five. My God, not five. Little did I know then just how much of a profound effect that abuse would have on the rest of my life, or how it would shape the person I am today.

I was born Yvonne Jeffries on 17 September 1966 at Perth Royal Infirmary, the first child of parents William and Jean Jeffries. My first home was at Fortingall Place in Perth, but I don't remember it at all and, if truth be told, when I pass that street today I don't even know which house I was born into. We didn't stay there long. In fact, we didn't stay together as a family for very long either. Dad walked out and abandoned us within a year, leaving Mum to fend for herself as a single mother. She struggled and at weekends

I went to live with my Auntie Betty, who was Mum's sister, and Uncle George to give her some respite.

It's strange, because I have very few memories of my time with Mum when I was growing up. I can remember fragments, such as her blonde hair, which towered above her in a 1960s style, and how she would always dress very conservatively. Old-fashioned, if you like. She was a clean and tidy person too, which wasn't a surprise, given that she worked as a cleaner for a bus company. Apart from this, though, I can recall very little else about my mum when I was a girl. However, I do remember one occasion when I sparked a full-scale emergency by going missing from home. Well, everyone thought I was missing. I was only about four years old and was living with Mum and, by that time, my grandmother in a flat in Perth, and I had become friendly with Pauline, the little girl next door. The pair of us would get together in the stairwell and play with our dolls and prams, as girls do, but one day we decided to go for a walk without telling anyone. We walked. And walked. And walked. Before long, the police were looking for us. Hours passed, but Pauline and I didn't think we were doing anything wrong – the babies simply needed a walk. When the police eventually found us and took us home, Mum said she didn't know whether to thump me or kiss me. It's a fond memory but, sadly, the only one I have left.

I'm not sure why I don't have cherished family stories like everyone else or why I've blanked Mum out. I've had counselling over the years to see if that would help any, but it remains a mystery. It may simply be that the trauma I suffered at the hands of my uncle has resulted in my early childhood years being wiped entirely.

I do know that money was tight when I was growing up, and as Mum continued to struggle, the time I spent with Auntie Betty and Uncle George at their house on the other side of Perth became longer and longer. Weekends became long weekends and then there was the odd weekday as well until before we knew it I was almost living there full-time. My aunt and uncle didn't have any children of their own. They had been unlucky over the years, and every time Auntie Betty did fall pregnant she miscarried. It meant she always looked out for me as if I was the daughter she'd never had, and I got everything I ever wanted when I was with her. While life was difficult financially at home with Mum, my aunt and uncle were both working, and with no child of their own they were desperate to spoil me. Who was I to deny them? They would take me out to places I'd never been before and do things Mum just didn't have the money to do. I loved it. If I'm honest, it's where I was happiest.

Uncle George adored me just as much as Auntie Betty and so no one seemed to mind when he suggested taking me away on a summer holiday, just the two of us. I was only five years old. The pair of us decamped to a small family-run hotel in Blackpool and it was here that the abuse started. The trip to the seaside became an annual excursion after that, sometimes for two full weeks, and by the fourth or fifth time I knew what the plan was going to be before we got there. During the day I would get treats and be allowed whatever I wanted. All I had to do in return was share a double bed with my uncle and give him what he wanted at night, and then keep my mouth shut.

The abuse was intense during these holidays – there was easy access for him and no one to watch over me. People who know about my past have often asked if I dreaded going away with Uncle George. The truth is I didn't. The abuse became part of normal daily life for me and I didn't know anything different; I didn't see what the issue was. Yes, it hurt to begin with, but I physically adapted and never for a moment did I imagine that this experience wasn't happening to every other little girl.

Mum was beginning to build a new life for herself by then and, with me away part of the week living at Auntie Betty's house, she had managed to fall in love and remarry. When I was 11, she took the decision to move to Hastings with her new husband, and I went with them. However, I really didn't get on with my new stepfather and I struggled to adapt to life on the south coast of England. After only six months away from Perth, I was truly miserable, so when Auntie Betty offered me the chance to return to Scotland to live with her permanently, I was delighted.

After years of staying on an ad hoc basis, 55 May Place in Perth, with its red door and my cat called Lucky, became my home in the spring of 1979. It was an end-terrace three-bedroom house on a council estate in the North Muirton area of the city, and I loved it.

My aunt and uncle both worked long shifts. Uncle George was a school janitor while Auntie Betty was a part-time cleaner at a different school. She would have to start very early in the morning before the pupils arrived and then go back late in the afternoon. It meant that, at the age of 12, I found myself in charge of the house, and I did the housework, including the washing and the ironing, and a lot of the shopping. Even the arrangement of the furniture, such as our garish orange three-piece sofa, and where the ornaments sat in the living room were down to me. However, Auntie Betty's shift patterns also left me wide open to my uncle's advances.

The routine was the same almost every night. Most evenings Auntie Betty would retire to bed early, leaving me alone with Uncle George in the living room downstairs. I wasn't allowed to go upstairs to my own room because the noise would keep her awake, or so I was told. Uncle George would lie on his stomach on the floor resting his

19

chin on his hands as he watched television, with a glass of whisky by his side. The moment he knew it was safe, he would turn around onto his back and simply say, 'Come on.' I then had to lie beside him and undo his trousers while looking him in the eyes. He would often try to kiss me, but the taste of the whisky would make me gag. This only made him complain that I was putting him off, and he would then push my head down to his semi-erect penis to perform oral sex on him. Sometimes he would tell me to straddle him as he forced me down by the shoulders so that he could penetrate me. He seemed to get some kicks from that, as if perhaps he felt he was playing at being a rapist. And, of course, that's exactly what he was.

I would never struggle or put up a fight. It was a chore, nothing more, and once it was done, it was done. Uncle George then left me alone and I could go back to doing my own things. I didn't enjoy it, and the whole day at school I would anticipate it coming and wanted it over with as quickly as possible.

At other times, if I went for a bath, and we were in the house alone, he would unlock the bathroom door from the outside and climb into the water with me. Uncle George was almost caught once when Auntie Betty returned home unexpectedly. He quickly got out and put his underwear on and explained that he had gone into the bath to play with me. He wasn't lying about that.

I was a prisoner in my own home. Wherever I went, whatever I did, he was always there, lingering in the background as if just waiting for a moment to pounce. Even when we walked past one another in the hallway, he would have a grope. The abuse was constant. It was particularly intense during the times my aunt left us to visit a cousin, 40 miles away in Stirling, for the weekend. With Auntie Betty gone for two or sometimes three nights, Uncle George, who was a heavy drinker, would go to the pub, but he would give me strict instructions beforehand to be in the house for a specific time. I had to be there for him returning to do whatever he wanted with me. After that I was free to go off wherever I wanted and even stay out all night. That was my reward.

I had a very strange relationship with Uncle George. It was almost as if he was obsessed with me. When I went out, he would want to come with me. When I met friends, he wanted to go too. He wanted to be my friend, he wanted to be my partner, he wanted to be my lover. Yet he was my uncle.

When I was thirteen, I asked Uncle George if one of my friends could join us for our summer break in Blackpool. 'Yeah, no problem,' he said excitedly. In hindsight, I should have wondered why he was so keen for her to come with us, but I didn't realise until we got to the hotel that he wanted to abuse her too. At the end of the first day, he demanded we both sleep naked with him in his bed. My friend wasn't impressed and hurriedly put her pyjamas on. However, the next day Uncle George went to the joke shop and secretly bought itching powder to put into our nightwear. On the second night, unable to wear our pyjamas, we had no alternative but to sleep naked, and that's what we did. With him in the middle. My friend was horrified. She wrapped herself up in spare sheets and spat in his face whenever he tried to get near her.

When I saw her reaction, the penny finally dropped and I began to realise that what Uncle George had been doing to me was wrong. When we got home to Perth, my friend told her mother, and I remember being lectured about his unacceptable behaviour. I became really upset and pleaded for them not to tell the police or anyone in the family, because I thought I would be taken away from my aunt. The woman didn't tell anyone in the end, but my friend was forbidden from coming anywhere near our house. My uncle did tell my aunt about the girl spitting at him – his version of it anyway – and I was then forbidden from being friends with anyone who was dirty enough to spit. My friendship with that girl was over.

Uncle George became very manipulative after that. When I finally questioned him about why he was doing these things to me, he said, 'You started it. It's your fault. You climbed on top of me and were jumping up and down on me. You must have wanted it.' He was talking about when I was five, when I was no doubt doing what any little girl would do as they had fun with their uncle. 'If you tell anybody,' he carried on, 'you'll be taken into a home. Your mum doesn't want you, your dad doesn't want you, Auntie Betty won't believe you, and you'll get taken away. If anybody was to believe you, I'd be put in jail and you don't want that, do you?'

He was right. I didn't want him to go to prison. He was a highly respected member of the community and someone people described as a 'good bloke'. The suffering continued, in silence.

Looking back on it now, I should have told someone, but I believed every word of what he said then. I even believed it was my fault, that I had started it. There was no reason whatsoever for me to doubt it. People talk about the horror of abuse, particularly when it comes to children. For me, when it was happening and was part of everyday life, it wasn't horrific. It's difficult to explain, but when it has been in your life for years, it simply becomes normal behaviour.

Having said that, even if I had wanted to run away and leave my uncle behind, there was nowhere for me to go. Mum was down in Hastings, and I didn't even know who my father was, let alone where he was. In any case, I wasn't brave enough to run off and disappear into the night. Some teenagers pack their bags and head south to London, but I just wasn't streetwise enough. I wouldn't have known how to run away.

I couldn't confide in anyone either. I had been well warned by Uncle George that if I did tell I would likely be taken away. That was a real fear. I already felt rejected by my father for walking out on me, and I felt rejected by my mother even though it had been my choice to leave her in Hastings. In my eyes, she had chosen my stepfather over me. But I knew my aunt and uncle loved me, however they showed it. Love: it's all any child wants.

In many ways, it was the lesser of the two evils to stay and put up with the abuse than to tell and lose the very people that cared for me the most. It sounds crazy, but Uncle George was still a father figure to me, the only father figure I had ever had. Auntie Betty had also been like a mother, and I knew if I told anyone about him that it would have a huge impact on her too. She didn't deserve that. It was easier just to carry on and keep quiet.

I always thought my aunt would have been suspicious, but, amazingly, she was not. However, I later found out that another uncle had raised concerns about Uncle George. The two men had been talking and during their conversation Uncle George told my other uncle, my mother's brother, about his time in the Navy when he would go to Hong Kong and find young children for sex. He even boasted about 'having a six-year-old' as if it was something normal. My other uncle was absolutely horrified at the very thought of it and went to Mum and asked if she had any worries about my weekends away with George. 'Are you sure she's safe?' he had asked. Mum then turned to my gran for advice, but all she said was not to worry. 'George loves Yvonne; he would never do her any harm,' she had insisted.

Everyone thought the world of Uncle George: that was the problem. He was a gem of a guy, one of the proper pillars of the community. And he was, at least to the outside world. However, his marriage to my aunt was a convenience and nothing more. It wasn't a marriage. They weren't close, they never went out together, and they most certainly didn't sleep together. He had his life, she had hers, and that was that. The only time they were ever seen together was at family gatherings or at New Year, when they would always throw a big Hogmanay party. I don't know how much, if at all, the fact they never had any children affected their relationship.

No one ever suspected I was being abused, even at school, where I spent most of the day. I was a very shy and quiet pupil. I wouldn't say boo to a goose, so to speak, and I didn't have a lot of friends. But if I thought going to school would give me a welcome break from my uncle, I was very much mistaken. At night I was being secretly sexually abused in my own home; during the day at Perth Grammar School I was the target of the playground bullies. I was seen as the class 'good girl', the pupil everyone else called a 'swot' just because I happened to do well in subjects and was in the top section of all my lessons. To make matters worse, I also had a problem with my weight. I was in plus-size clothes even at school and it became a major issue for me. When it came to sports classes, we all had to put on really tight navy gym shorts and a white T-shirt that showed every bulge. I hated it. Well, I didn't actually dislike the physical exercise; it was simply what we had to wear that I couldn't stand. There was no way of disguising lumps and bumps, and my appearance only gave the bullies the ammunition they needed. School became a vicious circle for me: I didn't have many friends because I was fat, but because I had to deal with the bullies I would go home and comfort eat.

Some of the stupid rules kept by my aunt and uncle at home didn't help either. Pupils at school frequently called me fat and smelly, and as a result, I was desperate to keep as clean as possible. I thought to myself, OK, if I was fat then I wasn't also going to stink. However, the problem was that Auntie Betty and Uncle George didn't allow me to use the bath every day. They didn't deem it necessary. It meant I was forced to secretly take baths without their knowing, by running the water ever-so-quietly then cupping my hands under the taps, both hot and cold, to muffle the sound. I then had to get in and out as fast as possible, dry myself, pour cold water in the bath and dry it before anyone noticed. It was ridiculous, but it had to be done to make life easier at school.

The bullying happened every day for about ten years; there seemed no way of avoiding the name-calling and the jokes. However, one day it stopped after I got involved in a punch-up in the playground. At the time I was dating a boy called Robbie and was absolutely besotted with him, but I found out a girl from a nearby school had also been seeing him behind my back. I sought her out and punched her straight in the face before pulling her down to the ground by her hair. Everyone who saw the fight – the bullies included – just stood there with their mouths hanging open. This wasn't the Yvonne Jeffries people knew. By dating Robbie, this girl was taking away the only thing I had: I'd simply had enough of being second best, and the aggression just came flooding out. Things changed after that: when people realised I could stand up for myself, school life became so much better. Even the teachers turned a blind eye to what I had done, having watched me being bullied for years.

The thing I could never understand about the bullying was that I wasn't a swot. I bunked off school as much as I could and missed lessons I didn't like, but it still didn't make me cool and I only had a couple of real friends. It was easy to skip classes at Perth Grammar School in the

1970s; as long as you registered first thing in the morning, no one seemed to notice if you weren't actually there for the rest of the day. Most mornings I would go to Robbie's house, having first used this cunning plan of checking in as present and correct at school. We'd sit in his room and smoke, listen to music, play darts or give one another trendy Indian ink tattoos. There would often be some of his friends there too, and at times it felt as if everyone who was skipping school was in the sanctuary of Robbie's house.

However, the only place I truly felt safe as I hit my teenage years was in my own bedroom at home. My aunt had put a lock on my door to give me some privacy as I grew into a young woman, and inside my room was my space away from the bullies and away from Uncle George. It was a fairly girlie room, with lace and flowers, though I must confess I also had posters of the Bay City Rollers, AC/DC and Thin Lizzy on the walls. Oh how I loved Thin Lizzy. I also had a CB radio, which I used to chat with people until the wee hours of the morning. It gave me a way of being anonymous; I could be whoever I wanted to be. I had to be careful, though, because I remember the men on the radio – and they were always men – would ask for my location and I would have to lie. However, I could tell by the reading on the meter that they were getting nearer and nearer, so I often signed off abruptly before we ended up with gentlemen callers at the front door! It was all a bit of teenage fun for me, but who knows what these lorry drivers would have been after had they made it all the way to May Place.

Childhood was not a happy time for me, and the few quiet moments I had alone in my room were welcome respite from a life of being abused wherever I turned. However, it was impossible to escape my uncle for too long and his sexual desire only seemed to intensify as the years passed. By the time I was about 14, Uncle George was regularly telling me he wanted me to have his children. He was deadly serious. He had decided that once I was 16, once I was legally old enough to have a child, he would make me pregnant with his baby. In the earlier years he had made sure he was safe by always using a condom, but he said he didn't want to use protection as I got older. Being manipulative, he had even persuaded my aunt to take me to the doctor and get me put on the contraceptive pill as I reached my teenage years. 'We don't want her getting pregnant now, do we?' he had said to Auntie Betty. I was to tell the doctor I needed the pill to control my menstrual cycle. Uncle George made sure I took that pill every day but warned me that the moment I turned 16 he wanted me off it. For obvious reasons, he didn't want anyone else to know that any baby was his. No, that would be his dirty little secret. Instead, what he had planned was that I would be in a relationship with someone else but then suddenly fall pregnant to him. Uncle George wouldn't raise the baby but at least he would know that it was his. That was his sick plan, anyway.

Clearly he was ill. He had to be ill. I know that now. For any man to feel that way towards a child in the first place, he has to be pretty screwed up. But to then want to make them pregnant defies belief. I was absolutely determined not to let this happen. Uncle George had already taken my childhood; he wasn't going to take my first child too. It meant I needed to get pregnant by someone else as soon as I could. I had to beat Uncle George to it. I needed an escape.

2. A Way Out

▲▼

I first met the man who would become my husband in a dark and dingy nightclub when I was just 15. He was as drunk as a skunk. It was late 1981, and even though I was still at school and supposed to be preparing for my exams, I was already a Friday-night regular at the Riverside Bar. Tucked under Perth Bridge on the banks of the River Tay, it wasn't the most salubrious of places and was renowned for underagers. In fact, at times the dance floor resembled a school outing, but no one seemed to care. It was easy to get in – we all just showed up with the birth certificate of someone older. A friend, a relative, it didn't matter as long as we suddenly became 18. Doormen never asked for photographic ID in those days, and I'm sure they knew about the ruse, but they turned a blind eye. That said, when I was 15 I never really looked my age anyway and could easily pass for 18 or older.

By this point in my life, there was a little bit of a rebel in me. Perhaps it was as a result of years of abuse at home and bullying at school, but I developed quite a devious streak. I craved fun and I wanted excitement, but I didn't know how or where to get it. I also wanted to be within an adult community and be with more mature people who weren't likely to hurl cheap insults at me. I found that sanctuary in the Riverside Bar nightclub.

I never went out to get drunk: that didn't interest me. All I wanted was to have a couple of alcoholic drinks, a dance and a giggle with friends and to savour the atmosphere of a more grown-up environment. Auntie Betty and Uncle George didn't really approve and they tried to discourage me, but at the same time they seemed to understand my teenage needs. They set rules, though: I couldn't go out on a school night, and while I was allowed to head to the Riverside on a Friday and Saturday, I had to be home by 11.30 p.m. That was fine by me.

It was during one of those regular nights out that Jim came sauntering over towards me. He'd clearly had a few drinks and immediately started declaring his undying love for me.

'I'm going to marry you one day,' he said over and over again, slurring his words.

'You're drunk as a lord. Leave me alone,' I replied, but he was having none of it. He had decided I was the one for him and that was that: let's get married. What nonsense! I was flattered all the same, and said to him that if he came back to the Riverside the next night, sober, and told me again that he wanted to marry me then I might think about it. I was being flippant, of course, and was more or less having a laugh at his expense, but, lo and behold, the next night he returned. This time he was stone-cold sober, as requested. 'I am going to marry you one day,' he repeated.

I wouldn't say Jim was Mr Wonderful, but I did like what I saw in him. He was slim and nicely dressed, and with bright ginger hair he certainly stood out from the crowd. At nineteen he was four years older than me, but he looked very young. He had potential. More than that, the fact he actually came back that second night was a huge compliment to me, probably the biggest compliment anyone had paid me in my entire life up to that point.

Jim and I had a dance, and at the end of the night he offered to take me home. As much as I welcomed the attention, I wondered what he wanted with a 15-year-old. I may have been a rebel, but deep down I still had some common sense. This boy was 19 and I was 15. It couldn't work. On the other hand, my friends weren't shy in telling me to go for it. 'Don't be daft. He's loaded; he's got loads of money,' they said. They were right: Jim worked with a landscape-gardening company and at that time he was earning a fair bit of cash, but that didn't appeal to me at all. I've always thought money is just something that buys material things, so I told him where to go. We didn't exchange numbers and off he went, disappointed. I never could have imagined then that he would actually go on to become my husband and the father of my children.

Back at home, I'd had enough of Uncle George's abuse and I told him I was no longer prepared to be his sexual plaything. It had to stop. I was now 15 and was very much aware that soon he would try to execute his plan to make me pregnant. I had already been refusing more and more to do the things he wanted, but hadn't yet quite found the strength to say enough was enough. When I did tell him, Uncle George didn't take it well and begged me not to stop the secret trysts. One day he even broke down in tears at the foot of the stairs as he pleaded with me to have sex with him.

'You know I love you more than anything, so please let me make love to you just one more time,' he sobbed. When I refused, he proceeded to take £100 from his pocket and offer it to me. I felt like a prostitute. Up until that point I had always thought Uncle George's misguided lust was also an obscure form of love for me, although, sickeningly, he loved me like a wife or girlfriend, not as a niece. Now I knew different: I was nothing more than an object to be fucked whenever he saw fit. I was furious and repeated that it would never happen again.

After the confrontation, I managed to escape only the worst of the abuse. There was never any sex after our fight, but he would still grope me or try to climb into the bath with me. If I needed money for anything, such as a night out, Uncle George would insist the only way to earn it would be to satisfy him. In those instances I learned to do without, and it wasn't long before I also managed to find myself a part-time job after school to ensure I wouldn't have to ask him for anything again. In many ways, it would have been easier for me to give in and carry on as we had been, but I had to remain strong, however unbearable life in that house had become.

I still hadn't told anyone about Uncle George. I was too afraid. At every opportunity he would remind me of what was at stake if he was ever found out. 'No one will believe you,' he said repeatedly. 'And if they did, no one would want to be with you after what you've done. Plus Auntie Betty will be so upset and I will be sent to jail.' He was right. He was such a popular person I honestly did not think anyone would believe me if I confessed. I felt that I would probably be seen as some spoiled wee brat who was making up wild accusations for attention. I was spoiled, at least materially, and people knew that. I got everything I ever wanted. What they didn't know was that in return for it, I had to satisfy the sick needs of my Uncle George.

By early 1982, my school days were coming to an end and I was preparing for a life away from Perth Grammar School. Fortunately the countless missed lessons hadn't done me any harm and I did reasonably well in my exams, gaining seven O Grades and remaining within the top three pupils in my classes. I had hoped to go to college and pursue a dream I'd had as a little girl: to become a nurse. If truth be told, I had actually wanted to be a doctor, but as I grew up I realised I wouldn't get the required university degree and fell in love with the idea of a nursing career instead. I applied to a college and, with my seven O Grades, was over the moon to be accepted. Sadly, the dream quickly fell apart because Auntie Betty and Uncle George didn't have the finances to support me through a college course, so I had to give the place up and look for a full-time job.

However, I was determined to find a career similar to nursing. I wanted to care for people – perhaps because of the fact that no one was ever there to care for me – and make others feel better. At the time, the government ran a scheme called the Youth Opportunities Programme to help school leavers into work. First introduced in 1978 by James Callaghan's administration, it was expanded by Margaret Thatcher in 1980 before being replaced by the more famous Youth Training Scheme in 1983. Critics of the programme said it turned school leavers into cheap labour, providing them with just £25 a week, but I didn't care: it helped me find the job I remained in on and off for the next 20-odd years. And so it was that in October 1982 I started my working days as a care assistant at Almondbank House in Perth, a hostel for adults with learning difficulties. I was pleased to be earning money of my own, even if it was just £25, and finally feeling part of the grown-up world. Admittedly I was slightly anxious about the job itself, particularly because I would be working with vulnerable people. I'd actually heard rumours from some of my neighbours that the residents at Almondbank were all insane and dangerous, and it's fair to say I found the prospect of arriving there on day one terrifying. However, what I found when I started were some of the friendliest people I had ever met, but people who were in need of some support, guidance and care, and those were things I was more than willing to give. I loved being at work and found the job satisfaction to be great compensation for the lack of financial reward, and I learned a lot from the staff there, not just about how to care for people but also about day-to-day life in general.

Taking that job proved to be a pivotal moment in my life because within weeks it led to a chance meeting with Jim, the boy I'd turned down at the nightclub a year earlier. I had been at the Youth Opportunities Programme office to collect my wages for the week and on the way back stopped at a pub for a soft drink with a colleague. There, sitting inside the Clachan Lounge reading a newspaper, was Jim. He didn't look as smart as he had 12 months earlier, but I knew it was him.

'You don't remember me, do you?' I asked.

'Yes, I do,' he said. 'You're Yvonne, and I still want to marry you.'

We both laughed. He joined us for a drink and we chatted about how both our circumstances had changed since the first time we had met a year earlier. I had now left school and was part of a work training scheme, while Jim was no longer working for a landscape-gardening firm and was unemployed. It was a reversal of fortunes, I suppose. I actually felt a little bit sorry for him. He had come across as very confident when we had originally met in the nightclub, and that had intimidated me, but he now seemed quieter: shy, and not so full of himself.

We chatted about our respective upbringings and our parents, and I learned that Jim, whose surname was Collinson, was the youngest of a family of seven, and the only boy. I assumed that as a result he would be spoiled but discovered that wasn't the case. Jim stayed with his father in a small village just outside Perth. His mother had died when he was only 12 and he hadn't had the easiest of childhoods himself, living with a dad who regularly took to the bottle in an attempt to blot out the pain of losing his wife. They had very little money. Jim's father hadn't worked for years, and Jim had relied upon his sisters to buy him food and clothes as he grew up. I think his poor upbringing made me feel we would be able to understand each other better, that we were kindred spirits.

Certainly, as we talked I could sense a spark between us and we soon realised we had so much in common. It was the start of something very special. Things moved very quickly after that, and after only a few dates it was clear I had been swept off my feet. We went for drinks, and on one occasion he took me out to a Chinese restaurant. It was all new and exciting for me: no one had ever taken me out anywhere before, never mind to a fancy restaurant. More than that, no one had ever treated me so nicely, certainly not a man.

We saw one another as much as we could and I loved the fact I had a boyfriend. It was clear Jim was besotted with me. If I didn't know it that first time at the nightclub, I knew it now. He couldn't bear to be apart from me. I remember one night he called me from a phone box near his house and at the mere sound of my voice he became desperate to come to see me. He lived 15 miles outside of Perth at the time and wasn't a driver, so he thumbed a lift from strangers to get to me. We were head over heels in love.

We hadn't been going out for very long when Jim decided to rent a flat in Perth so he could be closer to me and a new job he had taken. It was a strange place in that he had his own bedroom and sitting area, but he shared the kitchen and bathroom with three others in similar bedsits. He didn't mind the inconvenience because it meant he was nearer to me so we could see one another even more frequently. For me, that also presented the perfect opportunity to get some time away from the prying eyes of Auntie Betty and my lecherous Uncle George.

In no time at all Jim and I were living together. It was a two-sided coin for me, though. Yes, I was in love with Jim and this was a big step for us, and I was very excited about moving in with him. But at the same time, part of me saw it as a means to permanently escape the clutches of my uncle. People did try to offer their worldly advice and tell us we were too young and that I was rushing into a relationship with a man I barely knew. However, I didn't think I was too young – I'd had an older head on my shoulders for years by this point – and in any case, I was in love with Jim. I have to confess that even if I hadn't been, I think I would have still moved in with him, so desperate was I to get away from May Place.

Naturally, my uncle didn't want me to move out. Why would he? He needed to keep me close, and he cried like a baby at the prospect of my going away with another man. With the benefit of hindsight, I genuinely believe Uncle George *did* love me, though it was clear that what he loved most was the thought of having control over me. Indeed the abuse – albeit more psychological than physical by now – didn't stop, and I couldn't escape my uncle even when I was with Jim. Any time I went back to visit Auntie Betty, Uncle George would be there and would try to get his wicked way again when no one was around. I always tried to visit when I knew he was out, or when I could be certain they would both be there, but sometimes I just couldn't avoid him. Worse still, he started coming round to the flat where I lived with Jim and attempted to force himself on me once more. I was now 17, and at the back of my mind all I could hear was my uncle telling me he would get me pregnant once I was in a relationship. It was a terrifying prospect. I genuinely didn't know if I would ever be free of Uncle George.

Jim didn't know anything about the abuse. I deliberately hadn't told him about what my uncle had been doing to me over the past 12 years. I feared what his reaction would be. Here was a man who loved me dearly, and I thought that if I told him the truth he would see me as a horrible and dirty person and would have no more to do with me. I mean, what man wants to be burdened with a girlfriend who has been abused by her uncle? I felt like second-hand goods. Looking back on it now, it wasn't a rational way of thinking, but it made sense to me at that time. I couldn't tell him. Not yet anyway.

When we first got together, Jim knew I was on the pill, but after we moved in together I told him I really wanted to have a baby. He took a measured and sensible approach to the topic, and asked whether we could afford a child in our lives and whether we would be able to cope. I said, 'When will we ever be able to afford it? Let's just do it now. Plus, you never know, it might even be a boy . . .'

I dangled the proverbial carrot in front of Jim. It was a sneaky tactic, I confess, but I was aware that the extended Collinson clan was desperate for someone in the family to have a baby boy. Jim's four older sisters all had girls after they fell pregnant, and I knew how much a boy would appeal to him. It worked, and the contraceptives were gladly put in the bin.

Jim and I often reminisced about that first meeting we'd had in the Perth nightclub and we laughed about the promise he made to marry me. Then one day after we had been dating for about eighteen months, he actually asked. The proposal wasn't exactly Mills and Boon. There was no romantic dinner by candlelight, no flowers and most certainly no way he was going down on one knee. Instead, we were sitting in the Mallard Bar in North Muirton when he put his arm around me and quietly said, 'See if I bought you a ring, would you wear it?' I asked him if that was a proposal and he replied, 'Well, I told you I was going to marry you, didn't I?' And that was it:

we were going to be husband and wife. I was going to be Mrs Collinson.

I was so excited, but I realised the time had come to be honest with Jim about my childhood. It seemed unfair to go ahead and commit to being together for the rest of our lives with me holding onto a dirty secret. Jim didn't appear shocked by the abuse; he said that he thought it was quite obvious that my uncle had a 'thing' for me and that our relationship was far from ordinary. I made Jim promise not to tell a soul about it and, as far as I know, he never has.

We eventually had a proper engagement party, hosted by Auntie Betty and Uncle George, and were inundated with toasters and kettles as presents. The night before the gathering, Jim took me out for a meal and made up for his earlier marriage proposal by going down on one knee and slipping a ring on my finger as he serenaded me with Andrew Gold's 'Never Let Her Slip Away'. That would have been fine had Jim actually been able to sing. I wanted to crawl under the table, but at the same time I loved being made to feel so special. We initially talked about holding the wedding in September 1984 to coincide with my 18th birthday. However, the discovery that I was pregnant soon put paid to that.

It was March 1984 and there were no home pregnancy kits in those days, so I had to make an appointment to visit the doctor to be examined and undergo tests. I remember the day well, in particular the rush of adrenalin as I walked into the surgery, a very old building in King Street in Perth. I told the doctor I thought I was pregnant and expected him to be pleased and welcoming, but I'll never forget his response. As he ran a finger down the calendar on the wall, he slowly said, 'Of course, you will be terminating, won't you . . .' It was a statement rather than a question, and clearly he thought that at 17 I was too young to be having a baby. However, I left him in no doubt about my plans. 'Absolutely not,' I replied. 'This baby is very much wanted.'

I left the surgery and went into the nearest phone box to call my mum and give her the good news, that I thought I was pregnant. There was a silence before she too said I had to get rid of it. It really upset me. Here were two people in the space of a few minutes trying to tell me to end the pregnancy now, if indeed I was pregnant.

Five long days passed before I was able to call the surgery for the test result. It was positive. We were going to have a baby.

3. Life Is Perfect at Last

Jim and I tied the knot on 2 June 1984 on a gloriously sunny summer's afternoon, having brought the wedding forward by three months in light of my pregnancy. It was purely for vanity's sake, I must confess, as I already had the wedding dress and wanted to make sure I would fit in it now that I was expecting a baby. We were fortunate with the weather because it had rained for three days prior to the big day, and it was pouring down in the morning when I went to the hairdresser's. However, by afternoon the sun had come out and it was a beautiful and warm June day. It was perfect.

We didn't have very much money and the wedding, at Perth Registry Office, was a quiet affair. I wasn't nervous as I set off from my aunt and uncle's house for the last time as Yvonne Jeffries; I was so excited to be embarking on a new chapter in my life with a man I dearly loved. However, when I came around the corner and saw a throng of people standing outside the registry office, all waiting for me, I became sick with worry. My stomach was doing somersaults. Many people see their wedding day as the greatest moment of their lives. It's supposed to be a dream come true, with everything planned to perfection. That wasn't quite the case for me. Instead, all of a sudden, being the centre of attention felt like the worst thing ever. I generally hate the pressure of being fussed over and looked at, and yet here I was, the blushing bride arriving at her wedding with everyone watching. It's sad, but at that very moment I just wanted it over and done with.

Most of the family were there. Despite some people having reservations at the beginning – mostly due to my young age – everyone was happy for me when the big day arrived. They all had grown to like Jim. Even Mum had travelled up from Hastings and I was pleased that she had made the effort considering we hadn't seen very much of each other in recent years. My cousin Fhiona was my bridesmaid, and although I was three months pregnant, I was married in white, in a lovely dress bought for me by Fhiona's mother.

The service itself was very basic; the registry office was too small for the traditional pomp and circumstance of a wedding. There was no rousing organ music and I didn't even walk down an aisle. It meant no one gave me away, as such – the room wasn't wide enough for that – though Uncle George was by my side as we came out of the wedding car.

When the ceremony was over, we drove to North Inch in Perth and posed for our wedding photographs by the side of the River Tay. The pictures weren't done by a professional photographer – we couldn't afford that – and we relied upon relatives, but I'm happy with how they turned out. Standing there posing with my bouquet of white feathers and red roses I felt that I looked a million dollars, and I did.

We didn't have enough money to go for a lavish wedding breakfast afterwards, so Auntie Betty cooked a meal for Jim and me, her and Uncle George, her cousin and the aunt who had bought me the wedding dress. Mum wasn't invited and that caused a lot of tension. Mum and Auntie Betty had fallen out some months before the wedding and hadn't spoken to each other since. There was an atmosphere for the rest of the day, but I tried to look like I didn't care – I was married to the man I loved.

We didn't have a reception after the meal either and instead we all changed out of our wedding attire and headed for a night out at the nearby St Johnstone Football Club bar. It was just an ordinary Saturday night at the venue and nothing special had been laid on, but to us it felt like the best wedding party in the world. Jim and I then spent our first night of wedded bliss at the Gables bed and breakfast, a nice wee place where my mum had once worked as a cleaner. Jim and I were both smokers at the time and for some reason in my handbag I had 200 cigarettes for us to share. Unfortunately we didn't have a lighter or any matches and it made for quite a difficult cigarette-free night. We had a good laugh about it, though. There was no fancy honeymoon the next day and instead we headed back to our flat in Perth, back to that shared kitchen and bathroom. Yes, all in all, it's fair to say it wasn't the most lavish of weddings, but I was Mrs Yvonne Collinson and that's all that mattered.

I loved the idea of being someone's wife and having already witnessed the effects of a failed marriage on my mother I desperately wanted my own married life to be a success. I don't actually know what caused my parents to separate and Mum has never gone into any detail. Perhaps they were just too young: Mum was 16 when she got married. Dad never made any attempt to keep in touch when he walked out on us, and the day he left was the last time I would have any contact with him for nearly 30 years. There was never even a birthday card or Christmas present from him. He simply waltzed off and started a new life for himself without us and never looked back. End of story, as far as he was concerned. Why he didn't want us I didn't know, and it hurt, of course it hurt. I often asked Mum and Auntie Betty what became of Dad, and I was intrigued about the man whose name appeared on my birth certificate. Where did he live? What did he do? What were his parents, my other grandparents, like? Why didn't he want me? I never got an answer.

When I discovered, via the telephone directory, that Jim and I lived not that far from where Dad's parents stayed, I often walked past their house on the off chance that I would find clues as to who my father was. I wondered if I would recognise him from the few photos that I had; I wondered if he would know who I was. I desperately wanted Dad in my life even though I didn't know him, and deep down I harboured a hope that one day he would come back to get me. I dreamed of this man sweeping me up in his arms and telling me everything would be all right. Even on the day I married Jim, nearly 17 years after Dad had walked out, I still hoped he would somehow show up and be there for me. It was pure fantasy and I knew it would never happen.

After the wedding, I couldn't wait for everyone to know I was pregnant. In fact, if I'd had my way I would have walked around with a big cushion up my jumper. I loved being pregnant and I wanted the world to know. Having a baby was at the forefront of my mind. I would wake up in the morning and the first thing I'd think about was how fantastic it was to be an expectant mother. I was bursting with excitement. Not everyone shared the sentiment, though. Uncle George was devastated when he found out I was pregnant to another man. He became very subdued and was clearly upset, and I could tell he was hurting inside. Auntie Betty was angry and harped on about me being far too young. I was just 17, after all. That said, I think she was secretly pleased because she'd never been able to have a child of her own, but she daren't tell me she was happy for me.

This baby couldn't come quickly enough as far as I was concerned. I wanted to get out there straight away and buy the booties, the pram and anything else I thought I would need. From the outset, I also asked everyone I knew to knit jackets and cardigans. I just couldn't wait to become a mother.

I had a fairly easy time of being pregnant, although I did have a bad case of morning sickness. If truth be told, it was more a case of morning, noon and night sickness, and in the early days I lost quite a bit of weight. On one occasion when I was ill I went rushing off to the doctor thinking my baby was going to be damaged, but he just laughed and said I had enough excess fat still on my body to feed three babies. He was just being honest, and it put my mind at ease.

I was only a few months pregnant when I discovered Jim had had a fling. I say a fling, but it was more a case of him having tried it on with one of his female flatmates. I was horrified and packed my suitcase and stormed back to Auntie Betty's house. I knocked at the door, but when my aunt answered, she wouldn't let me stay and sent me straight back to Jim. 'You've made your bed, now lie in it,' she said. 'You were warned about being too young, and now you're pregnant. Now get back.' We got over it and I tried my best to forget it had ever happened.

I had been working in a fruit and vegetable shop called Betty White's when I fell pregnant, having moved on from Almondbank House when my time on the Youth Opportunities Programme ended. It also doubled up as a fishmonger's and part of my job was to help unload the boxes of fish when the delivery lorry arrived every day. It was heavy work, particularly for an expectant mother. One day after arriving home from the shop I had a very heavy bleed and, fearing the worst for the baby, I went to hospital for a scan. Thankfully the baby was still there and everything was fine, but because there had been a lot of blood the doctors said there was a possibility there had been a twin that I had now lost. They couldn't be sure and I'll never know either way. After the scare, working at the fishmonger's became more difficult by the day, and the manageress eventually gave me an ultimatum. She said I either had to carry on doing the full duties of the job, including the heavy lifting, or leave. I decided to leave: there was no way I was going to risk losing my baby for a horrible, and foul-smelling, job I didn't enjoy anyway. I found myself back at Almondbank House doing evening work as a carer, and it kept me busy until the baby was due.

Jim and I didn't want to find out the sex of our baby, but we both had a feeling it was a boy. Jim's Christian name had passed down through the generations – he was James Malcolm Collinson, his father was James Collinson, his grandfather was James Malcolm Collinson and so on – and everybody in the family was hoping for a little boy to carry on the tradition. We didn't even have a girl's name picked out, so sure were we that we'd be blessed with a son called James.

During the pregnancy, all I was hoping for was that the baby would be healthy and would have a better childhood than I'd had. I wanted it to have a good life and all the things I had missed out on: that was my ultimate goal. It already had a mother who loved it and a father who would be in its life, unlike my own. This baby would have a happy, loving childhood. I didn't have any high expectations that it should grow up to become a brain surgeon or a professor or anything like that. Happiness was the most important thing, and I stand by that to this day.

The one thing I had already decided, however, was that my uncle would never get anywhere near my son or my daughter, whichever we were blessed with. I had to put on the pretence of his having to become a grandfather figure to the baby, since everyone saw Uncle George as the father I never had, and that was difficult. Privately, though, I was making plans to ensure that the baby would never be left alone with him. He would never change a nappy, he would never babysit and he most certainly would never take the baby overnight. Anywhere my baby was going to be, I was going to make sure I was always there too.

As the months passed, I often pictured myself as a mother and fantasised about what it would be like with a baby in my arms. I'd dreamed about it for so long. Apart from when I was a young girl and wanted to become a doctor or a nurse, the only other thing I had wanted to achieve in life was to become a mum and raise a family. I wanted someone to call my own, someone to love me for being me and someone I could love back. I also needed to make myself feel better by giving someone else a better chance in life than I'd had. Psychologically, I was geared up for motherhood and what it would be like, even if I wasn't entirely sure how ready I was for the sleepless nights and dirty nappies. I simply could not wait, and the further the pregnancy progressed the more desperate I was for it to be over soon. I even asked friends for hints and tips or any old wives' tales that might bring labour on early. The baby was due on 20 December 1984, but by November I was getting fed up with the waiting. We tried everything to induce the baby, including driving the car on bumpy cobbled roads, but nothing worked. Then a friend suggested something a bit more risqué: that Jim and I go to bed and do what we had done to get pregnant in the first place. We laughed, but it worked, and the very next day I was whisked off to hospital.

The labour was fairly straightforward: textbook, I suppose. In fact, only about four hours passed between the moment my waters broke and the birth itself. The only

45

issue was that the umbilical chord was wrapped around the baby's neck when it was delivered, but that minor drama didn't last long. It was Jim who noticed first: 'It's a boy, it's a bouncing baby boy,' he cried out before bursting into tears. We couldn't have been happier.

4. Motherhood

Little James Collinson was born into the world at 12.44 a.m. on 4 December 1984. Weighing eight and a half pounds, with blue eyes and a tuft of strawberry blonde hair, he was my bundle of joy. I say 'little' because he looked such a fragile wee thing in my arms, but the reality is that he was quite a big, chubby lad for a newborn. In my eyes, he was gorgeous and the most beautiful baby in the world. I'm sure every new mother says that, but I truly believed it. Jim was equally ecstatic and couldn't wait to tell the family, so he decided to phone around everybody he could think of, even though it was the middle of the night. Naturally they were all delighted for us, 2 a.m. telephone call notwithstanding.

Despite all my bravado in the months leading up to James's birth, I hadn't actually had many dealings with babies and didn't know how to hold him at first. I also had no idea about the basic tasks, such as changing nappies or breastfeeding or even how to bath James. Thankfully the nursing staff had lots of patience and kept me right in those first few hours. Holding my baby son close to my chest, it felt as if all my dreams had come true.

However, it wasn't long before the colour of James's skin was causing concern for the midwives: he had jaundice. It is fairly common with newborns, and James was placed under an ultraviolet light for a few hours to see if that would help. It didn't, and his condition worsened. We started to panic. My little baby looked so helpless lying there under this bright light wearing nothing but his tiny nappy and some pads over his eyes for protection. We weren't allowed to go near him or pick him up and give him a cuddle. The only time we were able to be close to him was when he was feeding, but even then he was extremely sleepy. As a result, it meant my first experiences of breastfeeding were not pleasant, and it became a challenge just keeping James awake long enough to feed.

As the days passed, James's condition didn't get any better, and the jaundice became so bad the midwives eventually had to pump breast milk from me and feed it to him through a tube in his nose. For anyone coming to visit, he looked quite a poor and pathetic soul. We were suddenly hit by the enormity of the responsibility we faced as parents and it was quite an upsetting period for us; our perfect bubble had been popped. The ordeal was only made worse for us when Auntie Betty sauntered into the hospital one day, took one look at the incubator and asked matter-of-factly, 'Oh my God. Is he going to die?' The honest truth was we didn't know, and within seconds I was a wailing mess. Things did look bad, and while I was given the option of being able to go home, I just couldn't walk out and leave James at the hospital all alone. Instead, Jim and I sat by his side all day, desperately willing him to wake up and get better.

We knew jaundice was a common occurrence, but we also knew about the potential complications and how it can lead to brain damage – or worse. However, much to our relief, James's condition did improve, and after ten days in hospital we were finally on our way home for the first time as a proper family: the three of us. It was an amazing feeling.

We were still living in Jim's bedsit with the shared kitchen and bathroom and, of course, it wasn't exactly ideal. Much to the annoyance of our fellow housemates, we took over the kitchen, what with all the bottles and the other bits and pieces we needed to keep James fed and happy. He was still very sleepy in the first few weeks after we got him home. Other mothers have said to me they wished their babies had been able to sleep as much as James during the early days, but I hated it, as I still worried that there was something wrong with him. In fact, I was so concerned that I used to set my alarm to go off every couple of hours during the night so I could get up and check he was OK, that he was alive and was still breathing.

It's fair to say I was being a bit overprotective, and eventually a visiting midwife told me off for mollycoddling James too much. On one particularly cold day I wanted to make sure he was warm enough in the house, so I dressed him in his nappy, vest and Babygro, a cardigan, a hat, a pair of mittens and three blankets. Oh, and the electric fire was on, just to be sure he didn't get a chill. The poor wee soul must have been sweltering, and let's just say the midwife was slightly taken aback. She began the lecture with a roll of her eyes. 'All you have to do, Yvonne, is check behind his neck, and if he's a bit sweaty, he's too warm,' she harped on. We checked and James was lying in a puddle of water. I learned from these mistakes.

I truly loved being a mum, and in those early days I enjoyed nothing better than strolling down the street pushing the pram to show James off. Even though we lived in a block of flats and it was quite a chore lumping it down flights of stairs, I loved that enormous navy pram and would polish it before every outing. It was gleaming and I was proud as punch: I wanted everyone to look at me, the new mother in town.

James was spoiled for his first Christmas, but who could

blame us? We were doting new parents and he was the only little boy in the Collinson family. I don't really remember much about the day itself, but I know it was one of the happiest of my life. We still didn't have an awful lot of money and we were living in that shared flat, but it didn't matter. I had a new husband, a new baby and we were together for our first Christmas.

That year, I forced Jim out to find us a real Christmas tree because Auntie Betty had never allowed me to have one in her house. Poor Jim was quite a sight dragging this enormous fir tree up all the flights of stairs in the block of flats. We were still finding pine needles for weeks afterwards. When the festivities were over, Jim refused to do the return journey back down the steps; instead, he opened the window and hurled the tree out into the street. He did look out first. Well, I think so anyway.

Like most new parents, we had our fair share of scares and near misses with the baby at the beginning. One incident in particular still gives me goosebumps. It was the first New Year's Eve after James was born, and my aunt invited us around to her house for the annual shindig. I was slightly concerned about the fact there would be people at the party smoking cigarettes, so we decided we would take James upstairs and put him in a bedroom and check on him every so often. Auntie Betty had bought a carrycot for James that Christmas and we planned to transport him in that to the party. The taxi duly arrived for us at our flat to head to the family gathering, and we locked up and headed downstairs.

The block of flats had an internal stairwell with a set of steep stone steps. Jim was carrying James in the new carrycot, but as he headed for the top of the landing he turned around, bumped into the wall or a door, and dropped one of the two handles of the cot. Out rolled James. With a thump he landed at the top of the stairs and narrowly missed tumbling down the lot. We panicked and I screamed, but he wasn't injured – he was swaddled and bundled so tightly with winter clothes and a shawl he literally bounced to a stop.

By the time we got to my aunt's house, I had changed my mind about putting James upstairs. There was no way I was letting him out of my sight after what had happened. He slept through the music and the laughter of the party, and right into the early hours of New Year's Day.

We moved out of the bedsit and into a place of our own in January 1985 after complaining to the council about living with others while raising a baby. However, our new home – a ground-floor flat in Dunsinane Drive in Perth – was very damp and cold and was in need of some modernisation. For starters, as you walked in the front door there was an old-fashioned indoor coal bunker in the hallway. The windows were single glazed with metal frames and would freeze on the inside during the winter months, while the wallpaper would fall off as quickly as it went up, due to the damp.

Nevertheless, it was much more spacious than we were used to and, of course, we no longer had to share. We had a kitchen and bathroom of our own, a sitting room, two bedrooms and a double airing cupboard that would soon become home to the next addition to the family. Jim and I had always wanted a dog, and a few weeks after we moved in, Duke, a black and white Labrador crossed with a Collie, joined our growing ranks. He was to be with us for 15 years and became very much James's dog as those years passed. When James was in his pram outside in the garden, Duke would lie under it to protect him, but our new pet was also a bit of a pest, because if anyone walked past he would bark and wake the baby up.

Jim and I soon adapted to family life. Gone were our late nights out, and we established a routine of early nights and very early mornings. As I said, I was prepared mentally for having a baby and I had bought in all the items I thought I'd need well in advance. What no one had told me about, however, was the bond that developed between a mother and her baby. I didn't realise how strong this tie would become. For me, it was all-consuming and James became my world. I never wanted to leave him, even to go shopping. If a neighbour popped round to the flat to look after him for a short period of time to allow me to run errands, I'd be anxious and would go to check he was OK the very minute I arrived back home. I felt the bond between us was so strong that I couldn't bear it to be broken even for a moment.

I can understand now why relationships and marriages can be placed under stress by the birth of a new baby. Mothers often just aren't interested in the man who happens to be the baby's father. All you care about is the little bundle that needs your constant attention. You have to love them and cuddle them and ensure their every whim is catered for, and if that means husbands, boyfriends or partners are pushed aside then so be it. It was the same for me. That said, my married life was still good. Jim was my soulmate, my husband and also my best friend. We had everything that we had ever wanted and we couldn't have asked for more, so it came as quite a shock the day I learned that baby number two was on the way.

After James was born, I had returned to taking birth control, but when he was about seven or eight months old I was forced to stop for a very short time – a few days perhaps – when I suffered a stomach bug. It seems this presented just enough of a window of opportunity for nature to take its course. This time when I called the receptionist at the doctor's surgery for the results of the pregnancy test, I refused to believe her. 'I can't be pregnant. It can't be positive. I'm on the pill,' I chastised her down the phone. A few days later when I came in to chat with the doctor, I continued the argument with him. 'Look for yourself!' he said, handing me a slip of paper. It was true. Jim and I were expecting again.

Second time around, it wasn't the best of pregnancies and I was often quite ill, not only with morning sickness but also with a condition known as placenta praevia. It's very rare and only affects half a per cent of all pregnancies. In simple terms, it means that the placenta grows in the lower part of the womb, beneath the baby, rather than safely above. It causes the weight of the baby to press down on the placenta, in turn leading to a danger that the placenta can rupture. It's not good news, put it that way, and can cause the death of the baby or the mother, or both. I spent a lot of time in hospital so I could be monitored as my pregnancy progressed, and poor James, less than a year old, was pushed to the side. The doctors wanted me to be admitted to a ward full-time from about 20 weeks onwards, but I refused to do it because I had responsibilities at home. They weren't happy and even suggested that I place James into foster care temporarily, so that I could go into hospital, allowing Jim and I to concentrate on my health and that of our unborn baby. I didn't want to do that and knew I couldn't leave James with Auntie Betty and Uncle George, so I simply ignored medical advice and stayed in the flat. I was aware of the risks, but I was not going to spend four months stuck in Perth Royal Infirmary. It was a wise decision, because I would have missed James growing from a baby into a toddler had I not been at home. For instance, I'll never forget the first word he spoke. 'Mummm,' he said. I don't think Jim was best pleased, but I was thrilled.

James grew into a chubby toddler and didn't walk so much as waddle. It's fair to say he was bigger than average for babies the same age, and he was much stronger than them too. He was always very strong for his age. In fact, the midwives often remarked on how surprised they were to find James trying to push himself off the floor weeks before he should have been able to. Later, when he was about two, he even managed to push a dining-room chair along – while I was sitting on it. No one really knew where his strength came from.

James was a typical wee boy who loved nothing more than going on his tricycle. Needless to say, he regularly got into mischief. One day he managed to climb up onto the arm of the couch, open the window and clamber out. I had been in the kitchen making dinner and heard a knock at the door. I was a bit puzzled when I went through to the hallway, because normally we could see any callers through the glass panel at the top of the front door. This time there was no silhouette. Imagine my surprise at opening the door and finding James standing there in his sleepsuit. Thank goodness the flat was on the ground floor. James would also often get up in the dead of night and decide he was going to have breakfast, a meal that would consist of custard powder, sugar and cereal. Worse still, it had to be spread across the kitchen floor and eaten where it lay. Then there were Jim's tropical fish, which would have to cope with swimming past TV remote controls, slippers, the odd ashtray and anything else little James could get his hands on before dumping them in the tank. Yes, that child was full of devilment.

By the time I reached the 30-week stage of my pregnancy, the doctors insisted I be admitted to hospital – or face being taken to court. I had no choice this time. Sternly I was warned that not only was I putting my own life at risk, I was placing the baby in jeopardy too. They were right, of course, even if I didn't like it. Jim was working full-time and couldn't get any days off, so James was packed off to live with one of Jim's sisters. It was a harrowing time for me; I missed my wee boy so much.

On 22 April 1986, Stuart William Collinson was born into the world by Caesarean section and three became four. Weighing 6 lb 4 oz, he was a smaller baby than James had been, and, unlike his big brother, he had ginger hair. He was gorgeous and I couldn't have been happier. I was kept in hospital for quite a while afterwards to recover, but, typical me, I was desperate to get home.

When I finally got back to the flat, I noticed things weren't the same with James to begin with. It felt as if that deep bond I shared with him wasn't as strong as it had been any more. Perhaps it was the new baby, perhaps it was a result of the length of time he had spent with his aunt: I don't know. When she came to visit, James would be all over her, showering her with affection. It felt like he had missed his aunt once he got home more than he had missed me when I was in hospital. It hurt, but I consoled myself with the fact he was only a little boy. In any case, things returned to normal with time. When I was expecting Stuart, I had wondered how this special bond, this mother's love, could possibly be shared between two children. I'd had an overwhelming love for James since he was born and I couldn't understand how I would have any more love to give. However, I needn't have worried; when Stuart came into the world, I felt exactly the same as I had when James was born 16 months earlier. I loved them both equally and there was no favouritism. They were my boys, and nothing could come between me and them. James was fine with the new addition to the family and there was no jealousy issue, like there often is with many siblings. Yes, he would poke Stuart in the eyes and do the kinds of things toddlers do, but he seemed to enjoy having a little brother.

It was shortly after the Easter of 1987 when Uncle George

took his own life. He had been found out, not for abusing me but for interfering with a host of other children. He was only 50. His downfall had started a few days before Easter when police officers were waiting for him to arrive home from work. They wanted to ask him about allegations a girl had made about him at the school he worked in as a caretaker. A distraught mother had called the police after her daughter came home and told her the janitor had 'touched' her private parts and that it had happened more than once.

Auntie Betty called me in hysterics as the drama unfolded. 'You'll never believe what these people are saying about your Uncle George,' she cried down the phone. Uncle George was taken away to the police station and formally charged, but because it was the holiday weekend he was kept in custody until the Tuesday morning, when the court reopened. After a brief appearance before a sheriff, he was released on bail.

When I went round to visit my aunt, Uncle George was standing in the kitchen washing the dishes. He turned around to me and just shrugged his shoulders as if to say, 'Oh well, that's it. My life is over.' I did my best to comfort Auntie Betty without saying too much, because I knew I couldn't really stand up for my uncle; I couldn't say these terrible allegations were likely all lies. I only hoped that she wouldn't find out what he had also done to me over the years.

By now, the scandal had already been reported in the newspapers, and Auntie Betty had to deal with malicious phone calls and the odd piece of hate mail arriving through the door. It was a difficult time for her and she tried to put on a brave face, but I knew it was tearing her apart. The next morning she went off to work as she always did. She felt it was better to stay active and take her mind off what people were saying about Uncle George. He waited until she had gone and took a batch of crushed-up paracet-amol, washed down with a bottle of whisky. When Auntie Betty came back from work a few hours later, he was unconscious. By his side was a suicide note.

The paramedics were still there when I arrived. I broke down and cried and cried. I found it difficult to stop crying, if truth be told. For the first time, the enormity of what had happened to me over the past decade hit me. At hospital, Uncle George had recovered enough to talk, but he didn't admit to any of his sins. He denied them to the last. He never told anyone why he took that overdose; I suppose he hoped he would have died and wouldn't have to face questions. I went to visit him, not because I wanted to but because it would have been suspicious and awkward had I refused to see him. He died in the early hours of the next morning.

After his death, it became clear that I wasn't the only child to fall victim to my uncle. There were others, lots of others, and in the end that's what had driven him to take his own life. He was a primary school caretaker and had been abusing some of the children. After that first little girl had told her mum what the janitor was secretly doing to her, more youngsters had come forward to make similar allegations. Uncle George didn't get a day in court in the end: he wanted to take his own life before the trial. Like a coward, he attempted to escape justice. Some months later, Auntie Betty received a letter from the Procurator Fiscal to say that had he lived, there had been enough evidence available to prosecute him.

I feel a great deal of guilt about this. I often look back and think, 'If only I had told somebody, it could have saved those other kids.' That's my fault. I know it was Uncle George's fault for doing what he did, but at the same time if only I had confessed what was happening in my house then he wouldn't have been able to do it to anyone else. It's one of the many scars I have, one of the many regrets I feel about growing up, and at times it eats away at me inside.

When my aunt asked me to accompany her while she said her final farewells to Uncle George in the funeral home, I gladly accepted. I had to see his dead body with my own eyes before I could believe it and accept that, finally, my ordeal at his hands was truly over. There was a huge turnout on the day of the funeral, and I was surprised to see so many schoolchildren there, under the circumstances. Auntie Betty struggled to make it through the service and was completely overwhelmed with grief. I didn't feel the same sadness, however. Instead, I was hit by an overpowering sense of relief: it felt like the whole world had been lifted off my shoulders. It wasn't just because I had finally escaped Uncle George's clutches; it was also because I now knew my own children would be safe. I had worried constantly about trying to keep a close eye on the two boys at the same time when Uncle George was nearby.

As the days passed after the funeral, I also felt a great deal of anger towards my uncle. He had robbed me of my childhood and done so many horrible things to me, yet he would never be punished for it. With his demise, I also now had no avenue to get rid of my frustration – I couldn't exactly go and shout at him. Ten months after his death, I started attending counselling: it was the only way for me to deal with what had happened to me. During the sessions, I was encouraged not to feel guilty, yet when I eventually did tell Auntie Betty the truth several years later, I still felt as if I was confessing to some adulterous affair. She wanted to know what he had done to me and where it had taken place, and she was curious as to why I hadn't told anyone. After that, it was very rarely mentioned again. Strangely, Auntie Betty continued to keep a photograph of George beside her bed and I never understood why. I wondered if she had known all along, though I will never know now: Auntie Betty died in September 2007 following a battle with cancer. Not long after my uncle's death, she was forced to move out of the house to a one-bedroom flat in Perth city centre. It wasn't the memories that forced her away, or the shame of what had happened, but the continuous hate mail and malicious phone calls that plagued her even months after Uncle George died.

Uncle George's death gave me the chance to stop and take stock of my own life. Yes, it had been difficult for me by any standard over the years, but I also knew I was fortunate with what I currently had. With a loving husband and two boys whom I adored, life was great. And better still, my uncle was dead.

5. The Boy James

James became a proper terror as he left his toddler years behind him. If he wasn't digging in the mud or destroying the garden, he was climbing on top of sheds and getting himself stuck up trees. He was a boy's boy; he loved nothing more than adventure, danger and a bit of rough and tumble. However, it almost cost him dearly on a number of occasions as he grew older, such was his seemingly magnetic attraction to trouble.

I'm not sure what age James would have been at the time, but one near miss in particular sticks in my mind. The council had been renovating houses on a street along from where we lived and had left a number of portable cabins at the building site, which they used as an office and a place to store their tools. In his wisdom, James decided it would be fun to climb up a fence and onto the roof of one of the cabins. He then tried to leap between them, only to slip, fall and inadvertently find himself wedged between two of the cabins. He was well and truly stuck, and we could hear him screaming from the other end of the street. Jim and his brother-in-law had to prise the cabins apart to get James out, otherwise there would have been an embarrassing 999 call to the fire brigade. James simply loved to climb. Put him anywhere near a fence or a wall and he would be on top of it, given half a chance.

In another scare, James tried, and failed, to balance on some razor-sharp chicken wire he came across. Why he attempted it in the first place I do not know, but, predictably, he fell and one of the metal posts holding the wire went straight into his leg, ripping the skin apart. James was never a whinger or a moaner; he was one of those hardy boys who would prefer to get up again and dust himself down rather than burst into tears, no matter how badly injured he was. So it was only when we saw the blood seeping through his jeans, and then the hole in his leg underneath, that we knew he was hurt. He was some boy.

Having two young boys certainly ensured Jim and I were kept busy and on our toes, but it was lovely seeing Stuart and James playing together as they grew up. That said, I think their dad was an even bigger child than they were and made sure he never missed out on the action. He was Mr Fun, the one out in the go-kart with the boys or playing with their toy trucks. I was the parent they came to for comfort and a cuddle, and the one for all the practicalities, whether it be cooking or taking Stuart and James to nursery. With my uncle now dead, I wasn't as overprotective of them as I had been in earlier years and I let them out of my sight a bit more often. However, I don't think I was ever fully content until they were with me and I knew they were safe. I suppose I was just being a parent like any other.

Before we knew it, the time had come for James to start primary school. He enjoyed interacting with other children, having already attended a pre-school playgroup three mornings a week, and he was looking forward to making new friends. I have fond memories of seeing James all dressed up in his new uniform for his first day at Goodlyburn Primary School. It was August 1989 and he was still only four years old. He was as proud as punch as he stood there in the hallway wearing his charcoal trousers, a grey sweater, shirt and tie, and a bomber jacket, with his school bag slung over his shoulders. He looked so grown up, even though he would be one of the youngest in his class. I had been dreading his first day for some time and it's fair to say there were lots of tears as I sent James on his way.

It was during this same period that Stuart began pre-school nursery, and every morning I would have to walk past the window of James's classroom on the way to collect him. James's teacher later told us that she always knew when it was 11.30 a.m. because that was when, every day without fail, James would leap up out of his seat and race to the window to shout 'Mum! Mum!' He was never content until he had seen me and had a wave back.

As innocent as this behaviour was, it became the first sign that James's concentration levels were not what they should be. During his first term at school, his teacher noticed that his reading ability was not developing as it should and that he had some difficulty in writing letters down. He had no such problem with anything creative: he was very good with arts and crafts, and loved making models or colouring in. The teacher had all his attention for activities he could do with his hands, but when he was expected to sit down and read or write he was lost and would start clowning around. It wasn't long before he got himself into trouble for distracting the other children, and the situation only worsened as the year developed.

We were aware that James was a boisterous young lad with a tenacity that would accidentally get him into sticky situations, but he had never done anything to hurt other people. So when he were told that he had been caught hitting other pupils and had been bashing cars with a stick, we knew it was out of character for him. Jim and I went for a meeting with his teacher, and she told us she was concerned he wasn't responding all that well to the subjects being taught in class. His reading was poor and he was writing his letters back to front. However, she wasn't overly worried yet and said it could simply be immaturity, and that James would soon grow out of it and catch up with the older children. It was a phase, she said. When we spoke to James afterwards, he said he was misbehaving because he was bored. The strange thing is that we had no such problems at home and he was always eager to learn and loved bedtime stories being read to him. To us, he was a bright lad.

Unfortunately, James's classmates didn't see it the same way and they were constantly teasing him and laughing about his not being able to do what they could. Children can be so cruel to one another, as I already knew too well. James coped by turning into the class clown. It was as if he thought that rather than being laughed at for his problems, he would instead give everyone in the class something to laugh about by being silly during lessons. It may well have worked for the children, but it meant he ended up in trouble with the teacher – again. It became a never-ending cycle.

If this wasn't bad enough, Stuart developed problems of his own for us to try to deal with. For whatever reason, he seemed more restless and difficult to please than other children his age: he could barely sit still for ten seconds and never seemed to stop running around. He never wanted to sleep, and it was even hard to get him to stay still long enough to eat his food. If I hung up clothes on the drying screen, within minutes Stuart would be hanging off it, having knocked everything over. He would also jump up and down on the sofa constantly, and anyone who came to visit us at the house would end up going home exhausted just watching him. It was non-stop.

Initially we thought Stuart's problems were caused by additives in his food, so we changed his diet. However, nothing worked and he continued to literally swing from the curtains. There was no controlling him. Jim would come home from work and I'd be sitting in floods of tears. I really didn't know where to turn or what to do next with Stuart. At nursery, the staff also made comments about his behaviour, and eventually, at our wit's end, we took him to the doctor. However, all he did was smile and say that Stuart was nothing more than an extremely active little boy.

It wasn't until he was about ten that Stuart was eventually diagnosed with ADHD: attention deficit hyperactivity disorder. It was Mum who had said she knew someone at her work whose son had ADHD and had similar symptoms to Stuart. I hadn't even heard of it, but took Stuart back to the doctor to ask if perhaps my son had this condition. Following various tests and clinical trials, a consultant confirmed he did indeed have ADHD and it came as such a relief to know that he was actually suffering from a medical condition, something we could put a name to. After his diagnosis he was prescribed Ritalin and it worked a treat. At a school parents' evening, teachers commented on the difference it made to his behaviour in class and to his learning. His life was transformed. The ADHD does still affect Stuart today, and he is very fidgety and on the go all the time. Unfortunately he doesn't take the medication any more, but that's his choice.

By the end of 1989, I was feeling so lonely without my boys at home with me. I had been with them every single day since they were born, but now they were both out for part of the day. I didn't know what to do with myself. I was still working, but often my shifts at Almondbank didn't start until after 4 p.m., so I would be alone in the house during the day with only the dog for company. It felt empty and there was no one to fuss over any more, no one to mother. I was so glad to see Stuart come home from nursery school in the afternoon, but I needed a more permanent distraction: it was time to have another baby.

It took until the late summer of 1990 to fall pregnant, but I was delighted to find out we were expecting baby number three, and hoped for a sister for the boys. I had always wanted a baby girl but was terrified of the potential consequences when my uncle was still alive. My dreams came true on Easter Monday 1991 when my beautiful daughter Claire was born, weighing 8 lb 4 oz. She had a mop of lovely ginger hair like her brother Stuart and the most gorgeous blue eyes I had ever seen. She was our little princess. My empty nest syndrome was cured, and Jim and I were back to sleepless nights and nappy-changing once again. I loved it. Our family was complete.

James's learning problems continued into primary three, and it wasn't long before Stuart, who had only started his first year in primary school, had to help his struggling big brother. By this point, everyone was expecting James to have overcome his difficulties with literacy and to be reading and writing fairly well, but he wasn't. His poor behaviour also continued to be an issue, and when it was time to do written work in class, he persisted in clowning around. Sadly, the senior teachers at the school weren't proving to be all that helpful and simply wanted to punish James for his misdemeanours. I had a major disagreement with one of them – a woman I thought should have known better – after she sent him home with a punishment exercise in which he had to write 'I am a stupid boy' ten times. I marched straight into the school and confronted her. Yes, James had problems; yes, it was a good idea to learn how to write by repetition. But there was no way he was stupid. I knew that for a fact. While all his friends were watching children's television and cartoons after school, James chose to watch the Discovery Channel. He was so keen to learn, albeit visually rather than by reading.

We did have a breakthrough towards the end of that school year, however, when James's teacher finally suggested he could be dyslexic. I didn't know very much about this condition or how to find out more about it, since it wasn't so widely recognised back then. That particular teacher was due to retire, and from her experience of working with children she said she could see the frustration I was having with James and recognised that I didn't know how to help him. She confided in us and said that many of James's own classmates were exacerbating his problems by teasing him or being unruly themselves. During a parents' meeting in May 1991, she even suggested that we take James to see an educational specialist and then find a better school for him. It was the best piece of advice anyone had given us, and we duly followed her recommendations.

After the summer break, James started the next academic year at Caledonian Road Primary School. It wasn't just a new school for him; it was a fresh start too. He loved it from the very first day, and while it was further away from home and he had to take a bus to get there, he settled in well. It didn't take very long to see that the change of school had made a huge difference to James. He would burst through the door at the end of the day desperate to tell us what he had learned in class. James was so much happier and he made lots of new friends, and it was clear the teachers liked him too. In no time at all, he was reading and writing fairly well, and he was being given homework to do for the first time. He also ceased being the class joker: he had realised there was now no need for the other children to laugh at him any more. Eventually we did manage to get James referred to an educational psychologist, but all he concluded was that he showed signs of 'dyslexic tendencies'.

Our little two-bedroom flat was quickly becoming a little too cosy for us all. By the time Claire was 18 months old, she was still sharing a bedroom with Jim and me. James and Stuart slept in the bigger room, but with their bikes, toys and bunk beds there was barely any space left to move, let alone put in a bed for Claire. We knew we had to get somewhere bigger, but when the council told us we might have to wait about a decade for a house, we took the decision to buy a place of our own. We were in a better financial position than we had ever been before, particularly after Jim found work as a hospital theatre orderly in Dundee.

The house-hunting process didn't last all that long, and by the spring of 1993 we had moved into 15 Colonsay Street in Perth. I had been in the house before when it was owned by a friend and I really liked its layout, so when it became available to buy, we moved quickly. It was a mid-terrace ex-council house and we bought it for about only £28,000, but with four bedrooms, it felt like a palace. For the first time, each of the children could have a room of their own, and Jim and I could finally get some space to ourselves. It was also close to schools and wasn't all that far from where I worked. It was perfect.

James, Stuart and Claire soon made friends with the local children and we got to know our new neighbours. We were the middle house in a row of five terraced houses. In the back gardens all the fences were low, giving the residents the opportunity to chat and have a sociable cup of tea. We often spent long summer days in that garden, catching up on the local gossip or sharing food with the neighbours at a barbecue. It was a very friendly place to live. That said, our row was also extremely unfortunate, because the residents of every one of the five houses ended up suffering some kind of sudden death or tragedy as the years passed.

By the time he was ten, James was beginning to show an interest in the military and in the Army in particular, and he said he was keen on becoming a soldier when he grew up. Where that enthusiasm came from I'm not really sure, but I'm certain he was influenced by the programmes he watched on the Discovery Channel. Jim's dad had been in the Army as a young man, but he was reluctant to share his wartime experiences, so we discouraged James from asking too many questions of him. However, James found an interesting source in our elderly neighbour, Alex, who had also served in the military. Old Alex had a grandson who was about the same age as James, and the two boys would play together when he was visiting his granddad. Alex wasn't able to get around much, having suffered a stroke, but he loved pottering away in his back garden. He would often chat to James about school and what he wanted to do when he grew up. I'm told his eyes lit up the day James announced he was keen on becoming a soldier. After that we'd often find him and James sitting in his garden as he recounted yet another tale of Army life. James was enthralled, hanging on every word. Years later, when James told him he was going to join the Cadets, Alex was the first to offer to show him how to lace his boots. Old Alex used to tell us he thought James would make a good soldier. We never doubted it, even then.

My cousin William had also spent many years as a serving soldier and was a more up-to-date source of infor-mation, and James bombarded him with questions about the Armed Forces whenever he came to visit. William loved talking about his military days and he enjoyed showing James some of the tricks of the trade, such as how to 'bull' his boots and iron trousers properly.

It was becoming clearer by the day what James's chosen career was going to be, and we encouraged his curiosity. We never really viewed a future in the Armed Forces as a negative thing; we didn't immediately think of war and conflict. Yes, we knew it could be risky, but if that's what

James wanted to do, then good on him. Jim and I did chat with him about possible other jobs and James toyed with the idea of becoming a mechanic, but nothing stirred his passion more than the thought of being a soldier in the British Army.

At the age of 12, he couldn't wait any longer. The local Black Watch Army Cadet office was just along the road from James's school and, unbeknown to me and his dad, he popped in and signed up. Just like that. He wasn't even officially old enough to become a Cadet, but he lied on the form and said he was the required 13 years old. James was always a big lad for his years, so they had no cause to disbelieve him. When we found out, we gave him a telling off for lying, but we didn't lecture him or get him into trouble for joining up without telling us – he was just so eager. In any case, who were we to stand in his way?

It struck me how much James suited the Army uniform when he put it on to go to the Cadets the first time, even if it was slightly too big for him. 'You'll grow into it, son,' I laughed. He didn't seem particularly bothered, not if the big smile on his face was anything to go by.

Thursday night was Cadet night, and it was clear James looked forward to it coming around each week. He revelled in being taught all the basics of Army life, particularly the discipline side of it, and he enjoyed taking part in parades and going on weekend training camps. I think he liked the camps more than anything else because they usually took place at former Army barracks, making the experience more realistic as far as he was concerned. He was so full of enthusiasm when he returned from those weekends away, a bag of muddy washing slung over his shoulder.

It wasn't long after James started at Perth High School that his dyslexia was finally diagnosed. While he had come on leaps and bounds over the past five years or so, his reading and writing were still deemed to be in the bottom

1 per cent of the population. He would spell words phonet-
ically and you could make out what he was trying to write,
but he was struggling with his reading. James was given
what was called a 'record of needs', which meant he was
allocated special one-to-one support in every class in which
reading or writing was required. He was also given a
portable device on which to record his words instead of
having to write them down, and he had a voice-recognition
computer in the house to ensure he could do his homework.
During exams he was also given a 'read and scribe assistant'
to help him understand. It wasn't additional help or an
unfair advantage over his fellow pupils, merely a person
to read him the questions then write down his answers
verbatim.

His learning was finally getting better but the extra help
he was given brought its own problems and, sadly, the
bullying and name-calling returned. James responded the
only way he knew how: with his fists. He wasn't an aggres-
sive person, but he could stand up for himself and he
found himself a frequent visitor to the headmaster's office.
On one occasion, I got a phone call from the school telling
me to come and take James home immediately for his own
safety. He had become involved in a fight with a boy who
was the leader of a gang, but instead of the usual fisticuffs,
James had picked him up by the ankles and bashed his
head off the concrete playground. His sparring partner
was semi-conscious and an ambulance had been called. I
just could not believe my James had done this. It was a
nightmare. I think I cried for Scotland that night. Things
had been going so well for James as far as his education
was concerned, and I thought he had gone and thrown it
all away. His punishment was fairly lenient, as it happens.
He was only excluded for four days and he was forced to
meet the other boy and shake his hand. There was no
lasting damage to the lad, and the funny thing is that he

and James went on to become friends, and he even attended James's funeral years later. After that incident, the other pupils accepted James was no pushover and realised he was a boy who didn't take kindly to abuse. The teasing subsided, James kept his hands to himself and he finally became a popular and well-liked pupil – especially with the girls.

Young James Collinson was a bit of a Casanova it has to be said: the ladies' man of Perth High School. He was never short of a girlfriend and he developed quite a following of females. Any time I saw him out and about, he would be surrounded by a string of girls and would have one on each arm. At times, it felt like he had a different girl for every night of the week, and I think he did. He was very active sexually, even though he was, strictly speaking, underage. I remember Stuart going into James's room and finding condoms in the drawer. He was horrified and rushed downstairs to tell a tale on his brother, but, much to Stuart's astonishment, I simply shrugged my shoulders and said, 'I know, and that's good. I gave them to him.' James and I had a fairly open relationship and he was happy to tell me things about his private life, so I was aware he had been experimenting with girls. As a parent, I felt it was better for him to be sensible and safe than to try to discourage any behaviour with the opposite sex and see him make terrible mistakes. He would occasionally bring a girlfriend to the house and we would welcome her into the sitting room with a soft drink and an embarrassing story or two from James's younger years. Squirming in his seat, James would laugh along with us and then 'thank' us after his friend left.

As school progressed, James's enthusiasm for the Army continued. Meetings with careers officers became pointless exercises because he already knew what he wanted to do with his life, even more so now that he was a Cadet. He had even gone so far as to decide that he wanted to be in a regiment or squadron that provided logistical support to troops rather than see frontline action. By the time he was 15, James had earned bronze and silver Duke of Edinburgh's Awards for achieving good standards with the Cadets, and he had risen through the ranks to become a sergeant. He was also regularly being praised, and everyone who knew him said he was a good soldier in the making. For a boy who had endured such a troubled school life and was known as an underachiever in the classroom, the plaudits were welcome and only cemented his desire to become a soldier for real.

My little boy was fast becoming a man, and we found ourselves having proper grown-up conversations about his future, with James speaking to me in his new-found deep voice. James soon discovered Queen's Barracks in Perth had a recruitment station, and it became his second home. He was still at school, but he was constantly in the Army office pestering the soldiers about what he would need to do and what he would need to achieve in his education to sign up for duty. He was so keen to fulfil his dream. Jim and I knew nothing about the military and couldn't give him any guidance or advice, so we encouraged his visits to see the experts. By the time James was 16, he lived and breathed the Army, and the desire to serve his country pushed him through his final exams at school. He passed, including English and Maths, and had done enough. He was on his way to becoming a soldier.

6. Soldier James

If James's life was heading in the right direction, my own was falling apart: my marriage was on the brink of collapse. The warning signs had been there for years, but Jim and I just didn't take any notice of them. We were both so dedicated to our jobs and making sure the children were the main priority in our lives that we forgot to make time for ourselves as husband and wife, and before we knew it we had grown apart.

My job at Almondbank House was to support people with learning difficulties, whatever they needed. The unit had 24 adults living there, and while, to begin with, the care staff did everything for them, from washing and dressing them to helping them in the toilet, the idea was to support the residents and slowly enable them to become more independent. When they managed to get flats of their own, we would visit them and continue any support they needed. It was a stressful job and very hands-on, as you can imagine. When I was offered the chance to take a more senior post as a team leader, with a bigger salary and more responsibility, I jumped at the chance. Why wouldn't I? I wanted to better my career, and having more money would certainly help out at home. However, it's fair to say I underestimated the extra pressure the job would bring and the effect it would have on my marriage. My shifts became longer and longer, and I started finding it difficult to juggle family life and work. Days off were spent catching up on shopping and housework, and there never seemed to be any time left over for Jim and the kids, never mind for myself.

At times I would be working 24-hour shifts, starting at 2 p.m. one day and ending at 2 p.m. the next, and then I would be back in at 2 p.m. the day after to do another stint. Sometimes I took paperwork home with me too, so even when I was off, I was still working. It was tough going. The shifts meant that Jim was left in charge of life at home, but when I got back from work I'd find the washing hadn't been done, dirty dishes would be piled high in the kitchen sink, and the previous night's dinner would still be in the oven uneaten while the remnants of takeaway food were lying about. Jim was a hospital theatre orderly and had more conventional working hours, so there was no reason for him not to have shared the load. Yet I ended up having to make the breakfast and get everyone ready for school before I went off to work, then when I came back from the 24-hour shift I had to clean the house and prepare dinner. It just wasn't fair, and I felt that while Jim and I were living together, we were leading separate lives. We were nothing more than ships that passed in the night.

We sat down and had a long chat, and decided we would try a weekend away as husband and wife, rather than as Mum and Dad, to see if we could rekindle our relationship. We were supposed to be going to Paris, the ultimate city of romance, having paid for a cheap break in the reader offers section of the *Perthshire Advertiser* newspaper. Sadly there wasn't enough interest in the trip from other people and it was cancelled at the last minute. So instead of looking out the French francs and preparing for a bit of *je ne sais quoi*, we packed our bags and headed to Blackpool. It turned out to be a very testing weekend and any hope we had of falling in love all over again was quickly dashed. Where previously we would have been able to talk for Britain, we often sat in uncomfortable silence. The chemistry between us had gone; our marriage was dead.

In October 2000, I was due to take some of the Almondbank residents on a much needed mini-break to give them some additional respite, but a few days before we were scheduled to leave, I developed a terrible cough and felt truly awful. I wasn't sure what to do because I clearly wasn't well enough to head away, but if I didn't go then it meant the clients would lose out on their holiday, and I would have felt guilty about that. At the back of my mind, I was also aware that, with the strain on the relationship at home, the break away from Jim might have done us both some good. Absence makes the heart grow fonder and all that.

I decided to go, but it was a mistake, and by the time I got home I was struggling to breathe, my lips were blue and I had an atrocious cough. Even getting out of bed left me puffing and panting like an old steam train. I was really quite ill. My doctor couldn't fathom out what the problem was, however, and sent me to hospital, where an X-ray discovered I had pneumonia and my lung had partially collapsed.

I was signed off work, put on a high dose of antibiotics and told to rest. Rest? How could I rest? I had a household to run, a full-time job, a family to look after and a marriage to save. I didn't have much choice, though, and as difficult as it was for me, I listened to the medical advice and took things easy. For once, I needed Jim to care for me and the children, but it soon became apparent that we had passed the stage of having any compassion for each other. My biggest problem with the pneumonia was that I couldn't breathe properly, yet Jim would sit on the bed next to me smoking a cigarette. As I lay in my sick bed, we drifted further apart than ever. It had got to the stage where we weren't really even friends any more. I had fallen out of love with my husband.

Unlike other warring couples, we weren't having blazing arguments or fisticuffs. Instead, we endured hours of awkward silence. The only thing we had left in common, it seemed, was the children, and even then we would disagree about them. Don't get me wrong, there were numerous attempts to reconcile our differences, if only for the sake of James, Stuart and Claire, but everything failed. There was no option left but to ask Jim if he would mind moving out on a temporary basis to see how we felt about one another when we were apart. It was an emotional time for us all, and I sobbed as I watched him leave the house, get into his car and drive away. James was standing by my side trying to reassure me, saying over and over, 'It'll be fine. It's for the best, don't worry, Mum.'

Although Jim moved out, we had an unusual arrangement that he would come back every day to see the children and stay for his dinner. His visits became longer and longer, and before we knew it, he had moved back in. However, he stayed in Claire's bedroom, and while we shared a house, we led completely separate lives. We came to the conclusion that while the marriage was over we could still be friends and continue being a mother and father to James, Stuart and Claire even if we weren't husband and wife. In many ways, we got on better than we did before.

However, in May 2001 we separated for good and I headed to England. I had met someone else. His name was Malcolm Heath and I had befriended him on the Internet as my marriage to Jim faltered. In the beginning our relationship was strictly platonic, and we talked about everything over the Web, including the breakdown of our marriages. Like me, he and his wife were no longer together and he had young children to care for. We chatted every night for months and discovered we had so much in common. Eventually I plucked up the courage to go down to Reading, where he lived, and meet him for the first time. I had a great weekend, and when I returned to Perth I found myself missing him. Our relationship blossomed, and he offered me a place to stay in exchange for my helping to look after his two sons. With the situation so bad for me in Perth, it made sense for me to move in with Malcolm, even though he was nothing more than a very good friend at that stage. However, after I moved to Reading we became more than friends. We fell in love.

At the time of the separation, Jim and I sat down with the children and explained why we had decided to split up, and gave them the choice of where they wanted to live: in Perth with their dad or in England with me. We felt it was important not to make them feel they had to 'take sides' and explained it was vital they made the decision for themselves, and that they could change their minds at any point. Claire, who was still only ten, immediately said she wanted to come with me to Reading, but the boys said they needed to stay in Perth. Stuart wanted to finish his education without changing schools, and James only had a few weeks left before he sat his final exams at Perth High School and set off on his new adventure in the Army. As fortune would have it, he already knew he would be based in barracks close to me in Reading once he signed up for duty.

James was nervous about the prospect of formally joining the Army because he knew he would first have to sit an entrance exam. He feared that the problems with reading and writing that had hindered him at school could now end his dream of becoming a soldier at the very outset. However, the staff at the recruitment office knew James quite well because of his regular visits and they gave him words of encouragement. They said that he could try the exam, and if he failed on account of his literacy, they would take it on board and seek some additional assistance for him to sit the test again. In the end it wasn't required, and in the summer of 2001 James sat the exam and passed first time. He felt such a great sense of achievement to have done it by himself: he was now going to be a soldier.

James joined the Royal Logistic Corps on 10 September 2001 and was posted to Pirbright Barracks, about six miles from Guildford, in Surrey. He was so happy; he was bursting with excitement. He phoned the next day from the camp as the atrocities in New York and Washington unfolded on television. 'We're on red alert, we're on red alert,' he said over and over. His adrenalin was going and I told him to calm down. 'But Mum,' came the response, 'this is what I joined up for.' The barracks had become a hive of activity, what with the uncertainty of what was happening on the other side of the Atlantic, and James was revelling in being part of it so soon. I had a chuckle to myself after that call, because James hadn't even started his training and yet here he was gearing himself up for frontline war, in his head anyway.

When James left for the barracks, I didn't find it all that difficult to let go. Many parents dread the day their children fly the nest, but I was surprisingly calm. After my uncle died, I didn't mollycoddle the kids as much as I had when he was alive and, within set boundaries, they were given free rein to do what they wished. I never kept the apron strings tied too tight; I felt that they had to learn how to survive and get on with things, even if life was tough along the way. When James was growing up, I knew that if he did want to be in the Army then he would one day have to go off and live in a barracks. Both Jim and I understood and accepted that. In any case, while James was at Pirbright – and later at Deepcut – I knew I wouldn't have to worry about him. What could I possibly have to worry about? He was in a highly professional training camp, he was the happiest we had ever seen him, we had faith in the Army to look after him and, besides, it wasn't as if he was going out to Iraq or anything. In fact, I don't think I was any more anxious about him than if he had gone to a college or university campus instead of an Army barracks.

James said he found the early training, known as Phase 1, straightforward and said he was already familiar with much of it because of his time in the Cadets in Perth. That didn't work to his advantage, however, because his previous knowledge made him over-confident and quite cocky about the task at hand. He felt he'd done it all already and wouldn't have to work too hard. Just as he had done at primary school, he then decided he didn't have to pay attention and would concentrate only when he wanted to. His plan backfired and he failed the course. The irony was that he didn't fail because of his reading and writing. Instead it was because he hadn't cleaned his rifle properly. James was 'back-squadded' as a result, which meant he had to miss graduating – or passing out, as it is known in the military – until he sat the exam again. He was devastated and questioned whether he was cut out to be a soldier after all. However, he dusted himself down and took his failure as the wake-up call he needed to move on.

James eventually passed out at the second time of asking, and he became Private Collinson on 18 January 2002. It was a special day for all the new soldiers, as they paraded in front of their loved ones. A pipe band played and all the recruits saluted as they marched past the sitting spectators. There was plenty of pomp and circumstance, and we loved it. When we saw James he was beaming from ear to ear and, in my mind, he looked ten feet tall as he paraded in front of us. He was resplendent in his formal attire, complete with white gloves, and it was with great pride that Jim and I watched our boy come of age. After the official ceremony, which also included a prize-giving for the best recruits, we headed back to the Officers' Mess for a more informal reception. We got the opportunity to speak to some of the officers looking after James and they couldn't have given him any higher praise. One of his official reports stated that he had terrific potential. It was a great day all round.

During Phase 1 training, the new recruits hadn't been allowed too much contact with home as they prepared themselves mentally for the Armed Forces. We had rarely heard from James, and it was only after his parade that he was able to tell us in detail about what his first few months as a trainee soldier had been like.

'Phase 1 training is where they break down the civilian in you, and build up the soldier,' James said.

'And, eh, how exactly do they do that?' I asked hesitantly, fearing the answer.

James went on to describe an arduous 12-hour night-time exercise that ended with a scramble up a muddy embankment. It was cold and wet, and he said that every time he attempted to get up the hill he would slide back down. When he did eventually get to the top, he said the sergeant taking the drill had barked at him, something like, 'Finally. At long last, you've done it.' When James hit back with, 'Well, I'd like to see you do better,' he was kicked all the way back down the embankment. I was horrified by what James was saying and was ready to march into the office and confront the sergeant the same way I had done with the school teacher years earlier. No one was going to bully my son. I was after blood, but James simply shrugged his shoulders and said, 'Mum, I deserved it. I shouldn't have spoken out. It served me right. I've learned my lesson and I won't do it again. It's what they do. It is how they break you down.' It was quite an eye-opener. Looking back on it now, I still view what that sergeant did as bullying and can't accept that this is how young lads should be treated, regardless of whether they are in the Army or not.

James was obviously enjoying Army life, and not only the drills or the fact he was living and working in a barracks. He also loved the social aspect of it, and the women he suddenly found himself surrounded by. After his passing out parade James only had a couple of weeks off before he was due to be posted to the Princess Royal Barracks to begin his Phase 2 training. Better known as Deepcut, the Princess Royal Barracks was also located in Surrey and was just a stone's throw from the other camp at Pirbright. With so little home leave, James headed north back to Perth to catch up with friends and spend some time in Glasgow with a new girlfriend whom he had met fairly recently, during his time at the barracks.

I didn't know anything about the Princess Royal Barracks except that it was where recruits went to carry on their training programme. James didn't know much about the place either, except that he'd heard it was a bit old and dingy, and that many soldiers saw it as nothing more than a boring holding camp until they progressed to their final posting. Nevertheless, he was looking forward to going there because the Phase 2 training involved being taught the trade he would eventually do during his Army career.

James wanted to see some overseas action in the future, but his short-term goal was simply to get a driving licence, and then his HGV licence, so he could become a driver/air dispatcher. These are soldiers who have a vital role in dropping airborne supplies and loads from a helicopter or Hercules plane. To James, it sounded quite an exciting job, because it could involve going to inhospitable parts of the world where land transport was impossible, or supplying Special Forces on covert operations behind enemy lines in the dead of night. In order to become a driver/air dispatcher, James was told he would be given his driving lessons at Deepcut, before being sent to the Normandy Barracks at Leconfield, near the town of Beverley, in East Yorkshire, to do the HGV part of the training.

Deepcut was enormous. Surrounded by green fields and partially hidden by trees, it seemed to go on forever and ever. It gave the impression of being a fairly nice environment, at least from the outside, and in many ways it resembled a sprawling university campus – except for the mesh perimeter fence and soldiers bearing guns at the gates. We never got the chance to go inside and see what it was like away from its public facade while James was there.

We heard from James more regularly at Deepcut than we had during his time at Pirbright. The regulations didn't seem as strict, and James had a mobile phone and was allowed to use it. He also had most evenings free and he phoned on a number of occasions to say he wanted to be picked up so he could come to my house in Reading for dinner. One way or another, I was in touch with him every other day, and while he never really passed comment on what life within the camp was like, he was keen to keep us up to date about how his driving prowess was progressing. James was very excited about getting behind the wheel and day by day he was edging ever closer to getting his driving licence. He also said he had discovered that the barracks ran evenings classes in English and had signed up so that he could improve his literacy skills. There was no doubt that everything was going well. However, James didn't like guard duty, and he moaned repeatedly about it being a tedious chore that entailed very little except walking the circumference of the perimeter fence and manning the gates. He also said it was extremely tiring, because a guard-duty shift lasted twenty-four hours on a rota of two hours on, two hours off.

That said, he knew it was part of his training, and however much he disliked it, he accepted it had to be done.

James was very proud of his Scottish roots and wasn't shy in telling his fellow soldiers he came from the fair city of Perth, about an hour's drive north of Stirling. During his first days at Deepcut, he befriended a number of other recruits from Scotland and, for whatever reason, they all kept themselves separate from the English soldiers. There wasn't any tension or ill-feeling between the groups, although there was regular banter between the nationalities, as you would expect. Nicknamed 'CU Jimmy' by his English colleagues, James was very much part of the Jocks, and happy to be so.

It was good to see that James was still his normal self and that having a job and being away from home hadn't changed him much. He was chirpy, chatty and full of the cheek we were used to. James really did seem to be enjoying the first few weeks of the new camp. It seemed to present him with a fresh challenge. He was learning to drive, he was gaining new skills and he had met new friends. He had also found yet another new girlfriend, called Kelly, having ended the relationship with the other girl in Glasgow. Life couldn't have been any better for him. The future was bright.

7. 22 March 2002

It was a weekend that started out like any other; it was the epitome of normal. On the morning of Friday, 22 March 2002, Malcolm went off to work while I stayed at home to look after his boys Ben and Stephen, then aged two and four. I had recently found casual work nearby in a home for children with disabilities, but I had the day off so instead I took Stephen to nursery before embarking on the housework. There were always bits and pieces to do around the house, and while Ben took an afternoon nap I pottered about tending to the hoovering and dusting, and I made up the spare bedroom with fresh bedding, as I did every time James was planning to come over. I had to be back at nursery to collect Stephen at 3 p.m. and then meet Malcolm outside before we set off to Deepcut to pick up James. As I say, the epitome of normal.

I'd spoken to James a few days earlier and he'd said he was coming to stay with us for the weekend in Reading. We saw more of him now that he was in Phase 2 of his training, and although it was his second visit in two weeks, I always liked to catch up and hear how his week had been. The previous Saturday, we had gone shopping in Reading because, with Mother's Day approaching, James wanted to buy me something special. I was touched when he picked out a necklace with a love heart on it. It was so sweet. I adored that necklace and never took it off for years, at least until my skin developed a reaction and I was forced to stop wearing it.

James went out that same evening, and the next morning he boasted that he'd been at a nightclub and the doorman had known he was a soldier just by the way he walked. It didn't surprise me. There had been quite a big change in James in the space of a few short months, from the nervy boy who had started his training at Pirbright to the man now at Deepcut. He'd also filled out physically; he was more masculine. He looked like a young soldier, and I think James was quite proud of the fact someone had noticed and associated him with the Army. However, to me he was still my little boy.

Malcolm and I arrived at Deepcut at 4 p.m., just as James had wanted, but he was nowhere to be seen, or so we thought. He was partially hidden by some bushes and was quite surprised to watch us drive straight past him. 'Just leave me standing here, why don't you!' he laughed as he got into the back of the car. It was typical sarcastic James. We had fully expected him to be staying with us for the full weekend, returning to the barracks on Sunday afternoon, and certainly he was armed with the large bundles of washing he always brought home for me. But after he got into the car, he asked if there was any chance of the laundry being washed and dried overnight, since he had to be back at Deepcut the next afternoon to do his guard duty, or his 'stag', as he called it. I'd have to work fast, I thought to myself.

From the barracks, we headed off to the supermarket to get some provisions, and when we got there James asked if he could have five pounds to buy some cigarettes. Wandering around the aisles at Asda, I asked him if he needed any spot cream; he was at that troublesome age and was plagued by teenage acne. We ended up getting him a few other bits and pieces to take back to the camp before telling him to go and fetch himself a couple of cans of beer for the evening, which he duly did. It was one of the most routine afternoons you could imagine.

Back at the house, we had our dinner and caught up on what James had been doing during his week at the barracks. He had just passed his driving test and was delighted to be legally able to drive, and he wanted to spend the evening researching cars on the Internet. James had high hopes of securing a Porsche or a Ferrari or something equally flash on the cheap, but Malcolm pointed him towards more sensible, and affordable, alternatives. We were pleased he had passed his test and we thought we might be able to pay half of the cost of a car for James, hence Malcolm and I were keen to avoid the expensive models! I would have loved to have been in the financial position to buy him his first car outright, but it wasn't possible, so this was the next best thing.

James eventually decided on a 1.2 litre Vauxhall Nova, and he and Malcolm tried to find one within a twenty-mile radius that they could go and see during his next weekend with us. They then searched for potential insurance quotes to give James an idea of how much he would have to budget and, all in all, it was a productive evening. James seemed satisfied he had decided on what his first-ever car would be.

At that time, Malcolm and I had a three-bedroom council house, and James enjoyed staying over with us, away from the rigmarole of the barracks. It had a lovely and bright open-plan lounge/dining room with patio doors that led out to a nice garden. We had a brown-spotted Dalmatian dog called Sophie, who adored James and would get terribly excited when he came to visit. James was fond of her too, and he liked nothing better than taking her on walks in the evening, no doubt having a sneaky smoke when he was away from the house. After having trawled the Web for cars for what seemed like an eternity, James took Sophie for a walk and then went for a bath. When he came back downstairs, he said he was tired after a long week and was going to have an early night. Claire was no longer living with us by this point – she had decided she wanted to go back to Scotland and stay in Perth after our last visit there – so James stayed in her old room.

The next morning, I was the first person to get up so I could make sure James's washing was done for when he headed back to Deepcut. Having had Friday off, I was due at the children's home to work a shift at 2 p.m., so, although James didn't have to be at the barracks until 4 p.m., the plan for the day was to take him back early, dropping me off at work en route. It meant the washing had to be done earlier than normal. James eventually came sauntering down from his bed at about 10 a.m., but nothing of note sticks in my mind about that morning. It was the same as any other morning that James was with us, in that he'd have a long lie, eat some breakfast and laze about for a bit watching television.

After a while, James went off to iron the uniform he needed for that night and seemed to take a long time over it. As I continued to fold up his washing, we chatted and the subject of guard duty arose. Out of curiosity I asked him more about what doing a 'stag' entailed. Again he said it was boring and involved going around the perimeter fence with one or two other recruits to check for intruders or any problems. He explained that only soldiers over the age of 18 were permitted to carry firearms, so he did his guard duty without a gun because he wasn't old enough. It didn't bother him, but I had concerns.

'What if someone has a pop at you, and you don't have a gun?' I asked, my motherly instincts kicking in again.

'Oh, don't worry, Mum,' James said. 'There is always

someone else there minding your back. You're never on your own; there is always another person with you at all times. It's the British Army we're talking about, not the Boy Scouts,' he added with a chuckle.

He then went on to explain that even if a soldier on guard duty needed to have an impromptu toilet stop behind a bush, he or she would be accompanied. It seemed fairly sensible, I thought.

James said he hadn't actually been due to work that night but had swapped the stag duty with someone else and was being paid £40 to cover their shift. By this point, he was being particularly precise about pressing the seams on his trousers. Then the truth came out. 'Well,' he said, 'if you are the best-presented soldier reporting for duty, and your seams are right and your boots polished just so, then you get excused. You're known as the stickman. If this happens tonight, I won't have to do the stag: I can go to the pub, and I'll still get the £40.'

James didn't enjoy doing the guard duty; we already knew that. However, it seemed that no one liked it. Nothing ever happened, and it was a long shift. It was the lowest-ranking job going and not the kind of activity you would willingly volunteer to do. Unless there was money involved, of course.

We were aware that money was tight for James. He told us so at every opportunity and was always trying to get a couple of pounds from me here and there. A few days earlier he had phoned me to ask for £100, saying he was supposed to be heading to Spain as part of an Army exercise and needed the money for spending at night if the soldiers went to the bar. I told him I didn't have £100 to give him and he sounded a bit deflated. We left it at that and I never gave it another thought – at least not until a few years later, when we found out the Army didn't ever have any trip to Spain planned. Money seemed to be one of the things James and I talked about frequently, and I tried to give him advice on how to budget better. It seemed to be working – well, I thought so anyway. I remember us chatting about his sister's birthday, which was approaching at the beginning of April. When he said he was due to be in Perth that particular weekend and was going to be able to spend it with Claire, I said I would give him a cheque to give to her, even though I wasn't sure if she had a bank account. However, James said he would instead give her cash and I could then pay him back the next time he came to stay with us. I mention this for two reasons: first, that James at least seemed to have some spare money from time to time, and second, that he was making plans for the future. These observations would prove vital in the weeks and months to come.

I loved being able to see James so frequently. It was one of the advantages of being only about 20 miles away in Reading, as opposed to in Scotland. I still felt a deep sense of guilt about having left him and Stuart behind in Perth when I first moved to England. To this day, it is my biggest regret. While James loved being a soldier, what became clear to me during his visits was that his life didn't only revolve around the Army. He often made plans to see his dad, Stuart and Claire back in Perth or to catch up with old school friends and go clubbing. At one point he was trying to convince his brother to hire a car with him and go 'cruising for chicks', as he put it. Stuart was looking forward to seeing his brother in a week or two. He had always looked up to him and he missed James being around at home.

It was clear that, guard duty aside, James was finding some of his time at Deepcut monotonous, and he yearned for weekends away from the barracks to let his hair down. Certainly he said much of his Phase 2 training involved little more than keeping his kit and his bed space clean and tidy, and to prove it he once sent us a picture of how spotless his bed was. I have to say I found that particular photo amusing, because I had spent years moaning to him about the state of his room at home.

Back in Perth, Jim didn't see as much of James as I did, but the pair of them kept in touch regularly by phone. James had spent some time back in Scotland over the Christmas break from Pirbright in 2001 and then again after his passing out parade, but he hadn't been home since he'd started at Deepcut in early February. I know he and his dad chatted on the phone the day before James came to stay with us, though, and it was a fairly lengthy call. James had boasted about passing his test and had sounded his dad out about whether or not he should buy a car in Scotland and then drive it to the barracks in Surrey. Thankfully Jim advised him against that, anxious that his son would be driving on motorways and negotiating three or four lanes of traffic having just passed his test.

James got on well with his dad, although his bond with him wasn't as strong as it was with me. As far as James was concerned, Jim and I fulfilled different roles as parents, and rightly so. I was there to comfort and mother him, while his dad was the one for entertainment and some laddish rough and tumble. James would often go for a pint with Jim, but he would never dream of doing the same with me.

It was shortly before 2 p.m. on 23 March 2002 that Malcolm dropped me off at work on the way back to Deepcut with James. I had been sitting in the front of the car, with Malcolm driving, and when we stopped I let James out of the back and he made a beeline for my empty seat. I leaned forward to steal a kiss and a cuddle from him as he passed, but he was having none of it. 'Get lost!' he laughed as he pushed away my advances. We weren't really an affectionate family and I only went to smother him as a joke, fully expecting the reaction I received. James was a big strapping lad of 17, after all. 'See you in two weeks,' James said before leaping into the front passenger side of the car. It was the last time I saw him alive.

8. 24 March 2002

It was Sunday morning and I was enjoying a rare lie-in when the peace and tranquillity was broken by the sound of the telephone ringing downstairs. At first I left it to ring out. I mean, how important could it possibly be this early on a weekend? It was only 8 a.m. I then heard the answer machine kicking in and a message being left. It was Jim's voice and there was great anxiety in his tone. Only a few days had passed since I had started divorce proceedings, and I thought perhaps he'd had a rush of blood to the head and picked up the phone first thing on a Sunday morning to chat about it. Somewhere deep down, he still harboured faint hopes of reconciliation. I rolled over and decided to call him later. However, within seconds the phone was ringing again. Whatever Jim wanted, he was desperate to speak to me.

'What is it?' I snapped, having sauntered downstairs and picked up the phone before the answer machine took over again.

'It's James. I have something to tell you about James. Are you sitting down? I need you to sit down before I tell you this. Please sit down. You see he's been in an accident. Last night he was in an accident,' Jim replied. He was talking superfast.

'What do you mean he was in an accident? He can't have been. We dropped him off at the barracks yesterday.

He was going on an overnight guard duty. He's fine. What on earth are you talking about?' I said. But Jim became increasingly more anxious.

'Yvonne, he's not all right, he's not all right. He's dead. James is dead,' was his response. It didn't make any sense. Jim was clearly wrong.

'Look, Jim, he can't be dead. I was only with him yesterday afternoon,' I insisted. 'Who is telling you this rubbish?'

Jim said he'd had someone from the Army at the door at 7 a.m. to give him the news, but I was insistent that a mistake had been made. 'I'll go and phone James myself and show you this isn't right, and I'll call you back,' I said.

At this point Jim was becoming quite irate and began yelling down the phone. He knew the message wasn't getting through to me. He screamed, 'YVONNE. JAMES. IS. DEAD.'

It wasn't the shock of being told my son was dead. I genuinely believed a mistake had been made and that I would sort it out and straighten out the mess. I mean, how could James be dead? We had only dropped him off at Deepcut a matter of hours earlier. He was going on a 24-hour stag shift that wouldn't even be finished yet.

Jim was talking, but, again, I wasn't really listening. 'Has anyone from the Army been to see you yet?' he asked.

'No, Jim. Why would they be coming? James is all right. Would you listen to me, James is all right,' I replied with a sigh.

We were going around in circles and this exchange between us went on for what seemed like for ever. Even though I could now hear Claire in the background at Jim's house screaming in distress, I said again I would go off and find out what was going on and get James to call us back.

At this point, Malcolm came downstairs to find out what

the fuss was all about. 'Jim is telling me James is dead,' I said flippantly, before rolling my eyes as if to suggest the world had gone mad. Confused, Malcolm just stood there with a shocked look on his face, but I still was having none of it. I was cool, calm and collected.

I phoned Mum's house to let her know about all the palaver, but she was already at work and I didn't have her telephone number. At that time she worked in a similar care home to me, so I called my former colleagues at Almondbank House in Perth to ask if they had a number for the unit where Mum was based.

'How are you?' said the cheery voice on the other end of the phone.

'Oh, I'm fine,' I replied. 'I'm just wondering if you have a work number for my mum. Jim's just called me telling me apparently James is dead . . .'

There was silence for a few seconds and then my former colleague started crying. I thought to myself, 'Why is she crying?' I still wasn't prepared to accept that anything had happened to James.

When I eventually called my mum's place of work, I think the shock and sense of disbelief was slowly beginning to hit home. I know this now, because what I said to the receptionist was, 'I need to speak to my mum, and what I have to tell her is that her grandson is dead. So, could you stay with her while I tell her?' It was starting to sink in. Maybe James was dead.

At this point, I didn't actually know what had happened. All Jim had said was that there had been an accident. When I was talking with Mum, I began wondering if James had been in a car with some other soldiers and had chosen to drive. Maybe he had tried to show off with his new licence and had been in a crash. That would have been typical bloody James.

I was very agitated for the rest of that morning. My

heart was pounding and I had to keep busy. I still wasn't convinced James was dead, if I'm honest about it. I tried calling his mobile phone several times, but it rang out. I never left a message, but I kept trying it over and over and over. I kept my phone beside me throughout the day and still fully expected him to call back once he realised he had so many missed calls.

I went into the washing basket and found a white hooded top belonging to James. It was the only thing I hadn't managed to get cleaned in time for his going back to the camp the day before. He had been playing football in it and it had a huge muddy imprint on the front that I couldn't get off, so he'd had to go back to the barracks without it. He had left it with me to use some stain remover on it and then rewash so he would have it clean to wear next time he visited. I took it from the basket and started washing it by hand, and as I rubbed and rubbed, the mark eventually came off it. I rinsed it out, then took it outside and threw it in the bin. I don't know why I did that.

At about 11 a.m., I started getting ready to go to work, as I was due on a 2 p.m. shift. Malcolm stared at me as if I had gone crazy, but I couldn't understand why. It was a normal working day after all. When I came out of the shower, I could hear Malcolm downstairs crying on the phone to his parents, telling them the supposed news. He must have been bemused by my behaviour. But the thing is, part of me was numb with disbelief and part of me simply refused to believe it was true, so in my eyes there was no reason for me not to go to work. James's guard-duty stint was due to end soon and I was sure he'd call back.

When he came off the phone, Malcolm told me he had already called my work to tell them I wasn't going in. Instead, he said we were both going to head to his parents' to get out of the house for a while. When we got there, I became even more agitated than I had been at home. They wanted to hug me and were offering their condolences, but I didn't know what to say to them. No one would believe that there had been a terrible mistake; no one would listen. I had wanted to stay busy so I could block out what people were trying to tell me about James, and I didn't want to talk about it, whereas they did. I had to get back to my own house.

The phone was ringing again as we walked in the front door. It was Jim again. He said he'd had another visit from an Army officer and had a bit more information on what had seemingly occurred. James had been shot, he said. My mind was racing, but I still didn't believe that something had actually happened to him. It was only 24 hours earlier that he had been telling me he didn't have a gun, and during guard duty there was always someone else there looking out for you. So how could he possibly have been shot? It had to be a mistake.

At that moment, I turned around and looked out of the front window to see two Army officials coming up the path. That's when it hit me. My James wasn't coming back. Before the knock at the door came, I broke down for the first time that day, and it felt like the tears were never going to stop. I sobbed and sobbed until I was struggling to breathe. My body felt like it had turned to jelly and I could barely stand up. I sat myself down while Malcolm went to the door.

The two men – a captain from the Military Police and a chaplain – offered their sympathies and handed me a letter of condolence from Lieutenant Colonel Ron Laden, the commanding officer of the camp. I didn't look at it at the time, but when I read it later I didn't learn anything new; it was full of all the usual general niceties telling us how highly thought of James was. The captain said there had been a shooting outside the guardroom while James had popped outside to have a smoke and that all of his comrades were too upset to talk about it. No one was quite sure what had happened, but it was repeatedly described as 'an accident' and something the Army would have to investigate to find out more about. It was so unclear and the circumstances were confusing. There was no mention of James having been armed or any implication that his injury might have been self-inflicted. We had so many questions, but the men couldn't, or wouldn't, answer them.

Above all, I wanted to know where James was. It sounds utterly ridiculous, but I had visions of his body still out in the open wherever it had been found, just lying there, with a sheet over him. I kept thinking he was all alone and needed his mum. I know I wasn't thinking straight, but I just had to see him. I felt I needed to hold his hand, to hug him and tell him everything would be OK and that I would sort it out, so I asked to be taken to him. The captain said he didn't know where James was and made no attempt to find out. It was most likely he would be in a nearby mortuary, he speculated.

We were then asked about what funeral arrangements we had in place: did we want James buried or cremated? However, I wasn't ready for this kind of conversation and politely told the men so. As he went to leave, the captain gave me a business card and invited us to call any time if we had problems or questions. The visit lasted less than 30 minutes, but the officer's parting words stayed with me for a long time. 'If you are contacted by anyone in the press,' the captain said, 'give them my details and I will deal with them.'

I couldn't understand why newspapers would be interested in me or my son, and I started wondering if there was more to what had happened than I was being told. Yes, I appreciate perhaps the captain simply wanted to shield us from the hassle and trauma of speaking to journalists, but, as I stood there holding that business card, I had the feeling there was something more to it, that something was not right.

I was distressed when the officers came to the door, but when they left I felt I had to pull myself together. I didn't want to be a wreck: I had things to do; I had answers to find. I needed to know what had happened to James.

It was about this time that the Army first started dropping hints that James had killed himself. I called Jim back straight away and told him I'd had a visit but was none the wiser on the circumstances surrounding the accident. Jim said he now had a visiting officer in the house with him, asking about the funeral arrangements. He also said the official had wondered 'what makes these young people do these things to themselves'. Determined to find out more about what had happened for ourselves, we dismissed his comment. James wouldn't have killed himself, for goodness sake.

Instead, I wondered what kind of accident James had been involved in that could have ended with his being shot. I envisaged dozens of scenarios in my head and thought perhaps someone had tripped up and accidentally fired the gun in his direction. I even wondered if the accident was linked to terrorism, given the fact the camp was still on heightened alert after 9/11. Suicide never entered my head. The visiting officers hadn't made any mention of James having a gun, and in any case, I knew he couldn't have had one. Just a day earlier he had told me himself that he wasn't old enough to carry a weapon on guard duty.

I went over the last time I saw James. I went over it and over it, again and again. I truly believe that if he had been planning to kill himself, there would have been a clue. For starters, I'm certain he would have given me that kiss and cuddle I had tried to steal from him outside the car. If his plan was to end it all, he would have known that was going to be the last time he was ever going to see me, and he would have wanted to say some kind of coded goodbye. But he didn't even give me a hug.

As James's mother, I'm also certain I would have been able to pick up on anything that might have been troubling him, or if there was anything wrong. You can just sense these things; it's a strange kind of intuition. But there was nothing. I felt nothing. The last time I saw James, he was his normal happy self. If anything, he was happier, because he had passed his driving test and was looking for a car. He was also excited about the prospect of going to the barracks at Leconfield to get his HGV licence, partly because so few seventeen-year-olds can boast one of them in their wallet.

The last memory I have of James isn't actually of the hug that never was. Instead, it's the smell of his aftershave. When he got in the car, it filled with this overpowering smell. I don't know what brand of cologne it was, but I would smell it for months afterwards, or at least I thought I did. It became James's smell.

I had now been informed face to face by an Army officer that James was gone, but I still could not fully accept it. I continued calling his mobile and repeatedly checked my own phone over and over in case I'd missed him trying to get back in touch. I must have tried calling hundreds of times. Eventually it stopped ringing out.

By late evening, Malcolm suggested we turn in for the night. It had been a long day. I went upstairs first to get ready for bed and noticed the door of the bedroom James had slept in was open, and I felt drawn to it. I could smell his body spray in the room and realised it was coming from the bed. I took his pillow and held it against my face, closed my eyes and imagined I was cuddling my boy. It was such a comfort to me and I wanted to take the pillow to bed with me, but I was afraid the scent would fade too quickly if it was disturbed. Instead, I placed it neatly back on the bed and closed the bedroom door. Everyone was then forbidden from entering that room for a very long time.

Malcolm asked if I thought I would be able to sleep, given the events of the day. But that night I slept like a log, and when I awoke the next morning I felt like everything that had happened the previous day was just a terrible dream. It was only when Malcolm turned around and asked if I was OK that I realised it was real. James was dead.

I started feeling guilty about his death. Had I played a role in it by allowing him to join the Army in the first place? Certainly when Jim and I signed the parental consent forms, we had no idea what we were letting James in for. At the time, we felt the right thing to do was let him do what was going to make him happy, and that was having an Army career. With hindsight, perhaps we should have waited until he was 18, when he would have been a bit more mature and worldly wise. Knowing what I know now, it was as if we sent him to his death: as if signing the consent forms was signing his death warrant. Had we made him wait to sign his own form, he might well be alive today. It is a regret that haunts me to this day.

I'm not sure where it came from, but I found an inner strength deep down inside. I had to carry on, and there was so much to do: I needed to find out what the Army had done to my boy. Jim, on the other hand, was a complete wreck. He couldn't stop sobbing.

On the morning of 25 March 2002, I was contacted by a coroner's officer. She wanted to ask me questions about James so that she could begin the process of formally identifying his body. She asked if he had any tattoos, birthmarks and the like, and then said she noted that he wore dentures.

'No, he didn't have dentures. James's dentist always said he had textbook teeth,' I said, as my heart started racing. Maybe it wasn't James after all.

'Well, we don't actually have dentures here,' the woman continued. 'But teeth are missing. It must have been the power of the gunshot.'

That was the first time we realised the shot had been to James's head. It came as quite a shock. The woman had been very matter-of-fact about it, and I didn't like what I was being told.

Again I asked to see James, but I was told I couldn't see his body for a couple of days because a post-mortem was to be carried out. It was beginning to sink in that it really was my son who was dead, but until I saw him for myself, I was holding out some hope. But more than that, if he was the soldier who had been killed, I kept thinking about him lying there all by himself. He needed his mum, and I needed to be there to give him a cuddle and keep him safe.

9. Suspicions

ᐯᐱᐯ

I don't think anything in the world can properly prepare you for identifying the dead body of your child. I was dreading it. Yes, I wanted to be with James and see him one last time, but I knew that the moment I saw him lying there lifeless then that would be it: he really would be dead. It was 27 March 2002, and little more than three days had now passed since the shooting. They had been three never-ending days of pain and uncertainty, three days of knowing James was gone but not being able to truly believe it until I saw him with my own eyes.

We eventually found out James's body was at Frimley Park Hospital in Surrey, which has a special Ministry of Defence Unit to treat military personnel. Malcolm and I were met at the reception by a coroner's officer, who took us downstairs to the mortuary. First, we were ushered into a little room, perhaps only slightly bigger than a cupboard, where I was given witness statements to sign. These were formal documents stating that James had been in the Army, and they also contained a transcribed account of the conversation I'd had with the coroner's officer on the telephone a few days earlier when we spoke about his teeth. One section of it highlighted the fact I had said James was in 'good spirits' the last time I saw him. As I read through the file, it was starting to sink in that the Army was concluding James had shot himself.

The woman said she would take me in to see James and give me a few minutes alone with him on one condition: that I promised not to pull back the sheet and uncover his body. I didn't know whether she was trying to warn me about something, and all of a sudden, I feared what was waiting for me. I didn't know if I was going to walk into a big room where someone would open a fridge door and pull out my dead son. I didn't know if James was going to be unzipped from a body bag. I could see the door through which I'd have to go in the next few seconds, but part of me now really didn't want to open it.

As Malcolm and I walked into the room, I could see James's body. He lay on a table, with his feet nearest to me. Above his head was a Bible on a stand. The table had been raised so that his body was almost up to my shoulder. He was lying there with his hands by his sides, though he was covered from the neck down by a purple velour drape with fringing on it. It meant only his neck and head were visible, and even then his head was covered in bandages. He looked like he was wearing a motorbike helmet made of hospital bandages. However, I could still see it really was James.

The first thing that hit me when I saw his face was that he had black eyes. That confused me, because he hadn't had black eyes when he had come to stay with us at the weekend. Had he been in a fight? His nose was also a bit swollen, but I assumed it was for the same reason he had black eyes. As I stood there, I didn't feel sadness and I wasn't angry about what had happened. Instead, I had this overriding feeling of numbness, quite possibly caused by the shock of seeing my son lying dead before me. Perhaps it was a psychological safety mechanism that had kicked in to save me from the pain of it all. I even found myself comforting Malcolm, who had tears streaming down his face.

In my head when I was planning that trip to the mortuary, I had wanted to give my James a final kiss goodbye. But I never did it. When I touched his face, it felt cold and damp. He didn't feel real any more. Between the bandages, the black eyes and a slightly distorted face, what was lying there wasn't my James. Yes, it was James, but it wasn't *my* James, and I couldn't bring myself to do anything except stroke his face. It was as if someone had made a waxwork dummy of him. 'What have they done to you?' I whispered over and over. Then I turned around and walked out. I was in there a couple of minutes and no more.

I asked the coroner's officer what had happened to James's face and how he'd come to get black eyes. She said it was most likely the trauma from the gunshot. As we prepared to leave, she asked us if we had heard of another soldier by the name of Geoff Gray, who had died at Deepcut in similar circumstances six months earlier. We had heard of him because of a newspaper report about an inquest into his death, which Malcolm's parents had brought to our attention the day after James died. The woman then said she had been contacted by this soldier's father to say he wanted to pass on his condolences as well as his telephone number. Mr Gray had said that if we needed someone to speak to, we could call him. Little did we know that when we did contact him it would be one of the most important phone calls we ever made.

By the time we left the hospital I could barely think straight, and I still couldn't piece together the bits of the jigsaw to get a picture of what had happened to James. First I had been handed a business card and warned the press might be in touch, and then the Army had strongly hinted that James had taken his own life. Now the parents of another dead soldier were trying to get in touch. What on earth was going on?

When I got back to the house, curiosity got the better of me and I called Geoff Gray's family straight away. His mum, Diane, answered the phone and the moment I said who I was she started crying. 'I am so sorry about your son,' she sobbed before having to hand the phone over to her husband, Geoff senior. He passed on his condolences and then said, 'Can I ask you a very personal question? When you saw your son today, how did he look?' I described what we saw in the mortuary and he replied, 'That's exactly how my Geoff looked six months ago. And presumably they are trying to tell you it was self-inflicted, just like they told me? Now, Yvonne, take my advice or leave it, but the one thing I have to suggest to you is do not have James cremated. Whatever you do, do not cremate his body.' When I said we were already making plans for a burial, Geoff said, 'Thank goodness. We made the big mistake of having our son cremated and I really wish we hadn't. Now there are things we may never know.'

We left the conversation at that. It had been great, liberating even, speaking with the Grays, and the doubts I had about James taking his own life were being strengthened. Now we had two soldiers dead in the same circumstances in the space just six months. Both had been shot, and both, it transpired, outside the same Officers' Mess. More than that, there were now two sets of parents unwilling to believe the deaths were suicides and harbouring growing suspicions about the Army. Something wasn't right.

On 29 March, Jim went to visit James's body when it was returned to a funeral home in Perth. Having asked the undertaker to leave him alone in the room, he took it upon himself to carry out his own secret examination of the body, or as much of it as he could access. It was a difficult task as James was ready for burial in his full military attire, plus rigor mortis had set in. Jim unbuttoned James's shirt and found some unusual marks on his neck and scratches on the back of his hands. Jim knew a thing or two about dead bodies because of his hospital work and, as far as he was concerned, what he found had alarm bells ringing.

The suspicion that something untoward may have happened to James was making it difficult to grieve properly for him. Things weren't adding up, and both Jim and I felt we had to keep looking for some kind of answer. It was an exhausting time for us. I would go to bed shattered by 11 p.m. each night and sleep soundly until about 2 a.m., when I would wake up because my mind would be trying to piece the puzzle together.

Back in Perth, Claire and Stuart were struggling to cope with the death of their brother. Claire was crumbling and shedding the most tears, while Stuart became very quiet and disappeared off into his own world. I worried about him more than anyone. He and James weren't just brothers, they were best friends, and the loss was particularly hard for him to take.

Army officials had been in touch every day after James died and any request we had was gladly accommodated. They were even taking charge of organising the funeral for us, and we passed on what we wanted, from the church it should take place in to the coffin we were after. Everything was arranged with minimal fuss. However, as far as the investigation into James's death was concerned the Army was quiet and barely any new information was forthcoming. We were told officers thought, perhaps, possibly, maybe James had borrowed the gun on the night of his death. It was all very vague.

The funeral was held on 3 April 2002 at the Riverside Church, not far from where the family home was in North Muirton. It was a newly built church and was fairly modern, unlike the older and more traditional kirks in the area, which we felt was fitting, with James being so young. It was a huge funeral, so large that police were forced to stop traffic, and there was not enough room inside the church for everyone who wanted to be there. People also lined the streets as our car snaked its way towards Riverside, and I remember Jim taking a sharp intake of breath and starting to cry as he saw the crowd. I put my hand on his back and said, 'It's time to be proud, Jim. Hold your head high and be strong. These people are here for our son. Let's do him justice.'

James's coffin, draped in the Union flag and with his Army cap and belt resting on top, was still in the hearse when we got out of the car. A group of soldiers formed a guard of honour for us as we walked inside the church, and then they went outside to carry James in.

The funeral was partly conducted by the Riverside's own minister and partly by the Army's padre, the same man who had visited me in Reading ten days earlier. I stared at James's coffin throughout and had to resist the urge to throw myself over it in order to keep him close to me. I knew where he was going shortly and I didn't want anyone to take him away. As for the service itself, I was so transfixed on that coffin that I confess I wasn't really listening, but I knew it was a moving and emotional affair. It went well, or as well as can be expected, apart from one thing that the padre said. 'We may never know how James's life came to an end,' he told the congregation. I remember thinking to myself, 'I bloody well will.'

At the end of the service, the coffin was carried out of the church by the same men who had taken James in. I watched as a woman I had worked with years earlier kissed her fingers and then put them on the glass window of the hearse. It was such a small, but poignant, gesture and I was reduced to tears. It pulled on my heartstrings.

I was filled with pride once more as we slowly made

our way to Wellshill cemetery in Perth, past the hundreds who had lined part of the route. At the graveside there seemed to be a mass of even more people as far as the eye could see. A group of Army cadets formed a guard of honour leading all the way to the plot where James would be laid to rest, and a solo piper played a lament as the soldiers carried his coffin towards the grave. Finally, one by one, the cadets saluted when James's body was taken past. They were only kids themselves and were clearly overwhelmed with emotion, and Jim had to stop to comfort a young girl who was completely overcome. 'All this for my boy,' I thought to myself.

I didn't know it at the time, but the soldiers who lowered James into the ground were his friends from Deepcut. I noticed that one of them became so emotional he almost toppled in after the coffin.

The Union flag that had been draped over James's coffin was folded precisely in a ceremonial fashion, and his hat and belt were then placed on top. A woman officer then marched over to us and presented Jim with this memento before saluting and turning away. As she returned to where she had been standing I muttered to myself, 'Is that all you have fucking left of my son? Is that it?' I was so angry. I know it is an Army tradition and is probably a poignant moment for many, but I wanted to scream at this woman. I didn't want a Union flag, a hat and a belt. I wanted my son.

After the funeral, we went to a hotel in Perth and mingled with many of the mourners who had been there, including some of the senior Army officials. The commanding officer of the barracks – the same man who had sent the letter of condolence – didn't attend, which surprised me, as it is common practice for him to go to funerals out of courtesy. However, the woman who had presented us with the flag came across and spoke to us. I didn't know who she was, or what position she held at Deepcut, but I heard her being referred to as 'Ma'am' so she must have had some seniority. She apologised for the fact that she didn't know James, but did say this should be taken as a good thing, because she was involved in the discipline side of the camp. James had never been in any trouble, so there was no reason for them to have ever met.

Jim and I wanted to speak with the pallbearers and thank them for carrying James's coffin, but we were kept away from them, and they were told not to come near us. We said to an officer that we wanted to buy the men a beer and he said that was much appreciated, but they then proceeded to sit together in the corner of the room as they drank their pint in silence before getting back on the bus and heading off. For some reason, they were not allowed to mingle with us.

There were other soldiers in attendance, including one who said he had been good friends with James at Pirbright and then at Deepcut. In a strange coincidence, it also turned out the pair had also been at the same primary school in Perth. He told us he had struggled during his early training days in the Army and that if it hadn't have been for the words of encouragement and help from James, he would never have passed out. Having been at school together, in Army training together and passing out side-by-side, the soldier was in utter disbelief to now be attending his friend's funeral.

Nothing was said about the circumstances of James's death during the course of the funeral. It seemed to be some unspoken rule not to talk about it, even in whispers. However, it only took until the next morning for us to start asking questions again. My cousin William, who had been in the Army, shared our suspicions that all was not well and came to Jim's house to offer his help.

'You can't just borrow a gun and shoot yourself,' he

insisted. 'Borrowing a gun isn't the same as borrowing a pen for the bingo, or a book from the library, you know. Not in the Army. It cannot happen.'

He had a point. I took out the business card given to me by the captain and handed it to Jim before asking him to call Deepcut to enquire about the current state of play with the investigation. Surely now, almost two weeks on, there must be some news. The captain was of no help whatsoever, though, and bluntly told Jim, 'There's one body, one bullet, draw your own conclusion. There is no investigation.'

We couldn't believe it. Why was there no investigation? What did he mean by 'draw your own conclusion'? Was he trying to tell us that was it, end of story? In short: yes, he was. The Army had been excellent up until the moment James was buried. In the days after the shooting, the captain had offered to deal with the media, while other officials were extremely helpful in arranging everything we wanted for the funeral. Now, however, it seemed they wanted to wash their hands of us.

We didn't know where to turn. Everyone was suggesting to us James had killed himself, from the captain and the coroner to the padre at the funeral, but we simply were not convinced. I knew my James and I saw him the day he died. He was not suicidal and he had no reason to kill himself. The Army was now even trying to tell us James might have been a bit down because, according to them, he had money issues and was upset by me and Jim splitting up. What rubbish. James was no different to most teenage children in 2002 as far as finances were concerned, not to mention his family situation. In any case – and this might sound harsh – I think of suicide as an extremely brave thing to do, especially in this case: to have chosen to blow your own brains out. It takes a strong mind and someone with courage. I don't think James was that brave.

Jim and I weren't prepared to accept the situation as it stood, so we decided we had to take matters into our own hands. Sitting around the kitchen table the morning after the funeral, we hatched a plan of action. It struck us that we hadn't had any contact from the local civilian police in Surrey. Surely the unexplained death of someone at an Army barracks would have prompted some kind of police investigation? We assumed they would be looking at it, but were concerned no one had yet been in touch. I'd always had great faith in the police in Britain, and if anyone was going to tell me the truth about what happened to my son then it would be them. It was their job to solve crimes after all. My task was to make a list of all the police stations near Deepcut and call them to find out who was investigating the death and get some information from them. While I made a start on that, Jim took care of looking through James's affairs and finances to ensure they were all in order. My cousin said it would be important for us to get a hold of all the paperwork held by the Army relating to the night James died, such as guard orders and other documents that were alien to me and Jim, and he said he would find out as much as he could using his sources on the inside.

As we sat at the table, there was a knock at the door. Jim duly answered it, and standing there were two women from the BBC's *Frontline Scotland* programme saying they were doing a special investigation into the Deepcut deaths. It only took about ten seconds for Jim to slam the door in their faces, telling them he had just buried his son and that he wasn't interested in publicity or helping any television documentary. We had been plagued by journalists in the days leading up to the funeral, and each time we politely refused to do an article. There was no reason for us to talk to reporters, none whatsoever.

'But this is exactly what you need,' my cousin said when

Jim threw the latest business card on the table. 'Think about it. You need answers and you want to find out what happened. Having someone like the BBC asking questions of the Army would be a massive help to you. They might be able to dig deeper than you and speak to people you can't get access to. The BBC could even turn out to be your biggest ally.'

Once again, William was right. Jim picked up the card and called the reporters back to the house. It was time to go public. When they returned, the journalists explained that they knew all about Geoff Gray and said they were beginning to link his death with James's. They also said their programme would cast serious doubt on the Army's assertion that both shootings had been self-inflicted. It was music to our ears.

We agreed to take part in the documentary, but I have to confess I was a little frightened, because I think deep down I actually wanted someone to provide me with evidence that James had killed himself, to prove that his death was his own decision and by his own hand. It terrified me to think someone else had killed him and how scared he would have been facing death at the end, and I was upset by the fact I hadn't been there for him when he'd most needed me.

I couldn't think of any reason for anyone to have murdered James. He was always the funny guy and seemed to be very popular at the barracks. I was convinced that it couldn't have been suicide, but I was equally convinced that no one would have wanted to kill him. Perhaps, then, it had been an accident or the result of someone larking about, I thought. Maybe it was even a game of Russian roulette gone wrong. But, at the same time, with Geoff Gray's death now at the back of my mind, I wondered how could it be that the same accident had happened twice? We didn't know it then, but this meeting with *Frontline*

Scotland would become one of the catalysts that started our quest for answers in earnest, and in the days to come the BBC journalists would arrange the first face-to-face meeting between us and the Grays.

When I returned to Reading, I began phoning around the police stations in Surrey, but no one seemed to know what I was talking about. I was passed from pillar to post, and I left message after message without anyone ever calling me back. It was soul-destroying. How was it possible that a 17-year-old could be found shot dead in an Army training barracks and yet not a single police officer had a clue about what I was going on about?

Things changed about a week later, however, after I agreed to do an interview with the *Guardian* newspaper. The article was going to be about how James's death was so similar to that of Geoff Gray, and it prompted the journalist writing the story to harass Surrey Police about what they had been doing to investigate. Wham. All of a sudden, police officials were calling me left, right and centre. It was as if they couldn't have cared less about us until there was some national media interest in them.

During one of the calls from the police, I explained that it was being implied that my son had taken his own life, but I wasn't convinced. I also queried why, if everyone thought James had truly killed himself, no one from the police had ever asked to speak with me to take a witness statement about his state of mind, as the coroner's officer had done. The lady on the phone said they 'had planned to' come and chat with me, and asked if an appointment in a week to ten days' time would be suitable. It most definitely was not suitable, in my opinion. Almost three weeks had already passed since James's death, and we were no further forward. More to the point, the longer the delay, the more chance any evidence that could show what had happened to our son would be lost.

A uniformed constable was eventually dispatched on 12 April 2002. He took a statement from me but appeared so uninterested I felt as if he had only been sent to pacify us and keep us happy. The constable did reveal that, unbeknown to us, Surrey Police had been at the scene on the night James died, but he said the officer who had attended was told by the Army that the wounds appeared to be self-inflicted. He'd shot himself: end of story. Thanks for coming, but case closed. I wasn't happy.

'So, these bullet wounds: how do you know they were self-inflicted?' I demanded.

'Well, eh, the Army people at the scene said—' the constable started to say before I cut him off.

'Did anyone take fingerprints from the gun?' I continued.

'Well, um, the experts tell us—' he stammered.

'What experts?' I asked.

'The Army,' he replied, slowly.

I couldn't believe it. It was now apparent that if the Army had no interest in listening to the concerns I had about James's death, then neither did the police. I had been forced to call around police stations of my own accord to find out if anyone was even investigating in the first place, and only got a reply as a result of interest from *The Guardian*. Now, here I was sat opposite a lowly constable: probably the same man Surrey Police would have sent had I called to say my cat was stuck up a tree. It was a disgrace.

The other thing that became clear was that no actual investigation had ever been carried out after James's death, either by the Army or by the police. The scene wasn't cordoned off, no forensic tests were carried out, no fingerprints were taken from the gun, and no one even bothered to question any eyewitnesses.

When *The Guardian* published its article over a huge two-page spread – and when the story was subsequently followed up by other newspapers – the contact from Surrey

Police intensified, and someone got in touch with Jim in Perth, even though he had never asked for anyone to call him. We were given the names of officers seemingly now investigating the case and we were told we would be appointed a family liaison officer.

It was a major breakthrough, and from the police more or less agreeing with the Army's position that James had killed himself on the night of 23 March, here they were suddenly telling us they would get to the bottom of how he died. The power of the press, indeed. I was pleased by this development, don't get me wrong, but at the same time it angered me, because it was obvious Surrey Police had tried to fob us off a month earlier. It seemed as if they hadn't deemed James's death important enough when I had gone to them asking for help, but now, after a number of damning newspaper articles, they had performed an about-turn. It was as if detectives were worried about what the media was saying about them, and they feared a journalist scorned more than a mother in need.

By mid-April I felt as if my life was on automatic pilot, and I dared not give any clues as to how I was truly feeling on the inside. The media interest in James's death was increasing by the day, but during interviews I was aware that I must have looked like some hard, emotionless bitch. Little did the journalists know how much I was hurting, how much the pain was burning inside me. I knew that if I turned on the waterworks each time I was asked about what had happened to my James, I would likely fall apart and never recover. I was under so much pressure and so much stress; I couldn't waver and had to keep strong. What kept me going was the feeling that I was doing something for James, that I was still able to protect him and continue to carry out the motherly role. In a strange way, while I was able to do this he was still alive, even if it was only in my mind.

It's fair to say the determination to find out the truth about James's death was taking over my life. I hadn't been back at work since the shooting, and Malcolm and the boys were taking second place to James and those needing my love and support in Scotland. I still loved Malcolm and my heart was with him, but I didn't have enough space for him in my life at that point. We chatted about it and, as hard as it was for him to take, he understood that being in Reading was making it hard for me to fight James's corner. I needed to be with Jim, Stuart and Claire; I needed to be where the focus of the media attention was. I had no option: I packed my bags and headed back to Perth.

10. The Quest for Answers Begins

It was on 30 April 2002 – a full 38 days after James was found dead – that Surrey Police finally announced a formal investigation into the shooting at Deepcut. Amid much fanfare and a great deal of grandstanding in the media, Jim and I were told by the police that every avenue would be explored in a bid to determine whether James's death was indeed a suicide, or whether it was a tragic accident or something more sinister. Senior officers insisted they would look at the case with an open mind and, under their police code of conduct, said they would assume it was a murder until shown otherwise. Years later we would learn this was utter nonsense, but at the time we felt things were moving forward. Despite my initial criticisms over the delay, the decision came as a relief and raised my hopes that I might now learn what happened on the night my son died.

Surrey Police also announced that it was reopening the investigation into Geoff Gray's death, with the two inquiries running side by side. I was pleased for the Grays after all they had been through, and they too believed they would soon know more about how their son had met his death.

We had a great deal of contact with Surrey Police in those first days, and we had meetings in Perth or in Surrey, as well as regular phone calls. We were also given updates from the two family liaison officers we now shared with the Grays. In fact, we saw those two officers – a ginger-haired Irishman and an older, and more sensible, woman – so often that as the years passed they went on to become family friends. They were good at getting us any information we were after and they were excellent at keeping us abreast of any developments from force headquarters. Nothing was too much trouble for this pair. The nice thing about them was that they were good fun. It may sound strange in such tragic circumstances, but sometimes you had to have a laugh and these two officers kept our spirits up. The Army, in the meantime, remained silent.

It was through our liaison officers that police officials admitted for the first time that no investigation of any sort had been carried out on the night James died. Following the visit from the constable on 12 April 2002, I already had suspicions that things had perhaps been lackadaisical, but I was shocked by the reality of the situation. After the shooting, Surrey Police thought the Army had the lead role in investigating what had happened, while the Army was under the impression that detectives were in charge but had nothing to do: it was 'a suicide' after all. In the confusion, no one did anything. That remained the case until 30 April 2002, when the police investigation was launched.

Now, I have only ever seen crime scenes in television dramas, but I would have thought that upon coming across a dead body, detectives would have automatically ordered a forensic sweep of the scene, or that perhaps they would have been on their hands and knees looking for bullets or mapping out the droplets of blood. I would have imagined, too, that the area would have been cordoned off and any eyewitnesses asked to give statements. None of this happened, and we learned that only six photographs were ever taken: no more.

What's more, on the night James died a wedding had

been taking place within the Officers' Mess. His body was found just a few feet from an emergency exit and was practically illuminated by the lights coming from inside the building, yet no one from the party was asked if they had seen, or heard, anything. Instead, they were given questionnaires to voluntarily complete if they thought they might have witnessed anything.

It would have been easy to become bitter at this stage, but we just wanted to move forward and do what had to be done to get the answers we craved. In any case, the signs were that the police were taking the investigation seriously, with Jim and I both asked to give DNA to detectives in order to ascertain if there was evidence of a third party having been at the scene of the shooting.

Within days of the police announcement, the media attention became relentless, and I think we had every Scottish newspaper and television news channel at the front door looking for an interview. We spoke to as many as we possibly could, because, with my cousin William's words still fresh in our minds, we felt that any outside help at all was a bonus. Every media outlet seemed to be on our side, and many of the journalists were shocked by the things we had to tell them. It made for juicy editorial as far as they were concerned, and it raised our profile with the general public. It was a win–win situation.

It wasn't long after this that the BBC *Frontline Scotland* programme we had been working on was broadcast, and it's fair to say it caused a bigger sensation than we could ever have imagined. Unbeknown to us, the journalists had found another two soldiers who had died at Deepcut in exactly the same circumstances as James and Geoff. Aired on 21 May 2002, 'Death at Deepcut' revealed that, in separate incidents just six months apart in 1995, Privates Sean Benton and Cheryl James were also found dead with gunshot wounds. All of a sudden, Deepcut became a news

119

story across Europe. Four soldiers, all dead from gunshot wounds, all in mysterious circumstances at the same barracks: it was dynamite.

After the programme, there was only one way to drive forward our quest for answers, and that was for all four families to join forces. We had to. There was clearly something wrong at the Princess Royal Barracks for four sets of parents to have suffered the same loss in the space of seven years.

We all met up for the first time on 10 June 2002 in the Westminster office of then Labour MP for Kingston upon Hull North, Kevin McNamara, who had taken a keen interest in the situation at Deepcut. He had arranged for a press conference to be held later that afternoon in order to keep the momentum going. Meeting the other families was extremely emotional, but we all instantly felt a strong bond with one another. After all, we had lost children in the same way and all desperately wanted to find out why. We compared stories and swapped pictures, and the tears flowed.

It was a brief meeting and after what seemed like no time at all, we were wheeled out in front of the press. I remember opening the door to a room and finding it packed with journalists, TV crews and photographers. Startled, and believing I'd stumbled into the wrong suite, I backed out. I had never seen anything like this in my life. They must have been there for somebody else, I thought. They weren't: it was all for us. I couldn't believe it, and I wanted to stand there and cry, such was my over-whelming feeling of relief. For weeks, Jim and I had struggled to find anyone to listen to our concerns, and now we had a room full of journalists from across Europe waiting to hear from us. By our sides were three other families who shared and understood our pain and wanted the same answers about Deepcut as we did. What's more, the room was also full of MPs who wanted to show their support for us. It was beyond belief.

In many ways, I think what was happening came as more of a relief to the parents of Sean Benton and Cheryl James than it did to us or the Grays. They had gone seven years without knowing what had happened to their children. Like us, they had been told their loved ones had killed themselves and that was that. Cheryl James's dad, Des, was very emotional at the sight of the journalists. He stood up and told the story of his daughter's death and at the end confessed that he felt ashamed to have given up his fight for answers. Seven years had passed and he'd simply let it go. He had had no choice. The Bentons were quiet, private people and they weren't very comfortable being thrust in front of the cameras, although they hoped the publicity would help bring an end to their own pain.

During the press conference, we made our first demand for a public inquiry into the four deaths at Deepcut. I laugh when I look back at that now, because I have to confess that at the time I didn't even know what a public inquiry was. We were all naive; we had taken advice from politicians beforehand and they said this was what we had to call for in order to drive a concerted campaign forward. Time after time, they all said the same thing – that we had to push for a public inquiry – so we thought, 'Great, let's call for one of them then.'

We looked like rabbits caught in the headlights that day, but I still think we got our message across well. Certainly I think the statement we issued summed up perfectly the way all four families felt about the Army. It said, 'We feel that the only way to address the mishandling [of the deaths] is to have the Army come before an independent board of inquiry. We need to find out who and what is behind the deaths of our children and who is conspiring to hide the evidence of [the Army's] misdeeds.'

We also told journalists that what had happened at Deepcut surrounding the four shootings was 'a cover-up'. It sounds very dramatic, but in our eyes that was exactly what it was, even if the Army had never been found guilty of any wrongdoing. By the time the press conference ended, we were on a high. We just couldn't believe that so many people were interested in our plight, and it was an amazing feeling knowing that the next day our story would be all over the newspapers as well as on television and radio.

What we learned more than anything was that there was a stronger appetite for us as a foursome than as grieving individuals, and that collectively we could achieve more than if we were on our own again. While each of us had lost a child and had our own tragic story to tell, we knew we had to work as one. The Deepcut story without three of the four families wasn't a story. It was only the four deaths together that interested the media, and we had to capitalise on that. We had become the Deepcut Four.

I was in quite a reflective mood at the end of that day. Fewer than three months had passed since James's death, but Jim and I now found ourselves caught up in a whirlwind. Here we were in London, addressing the UK media and doing live news interviews from the Houses of Parliament. It was surreal, and the only way I could deal with it was to pretend it was happening to someone else, as if I were watching it from the outside.

The day after the press conference, Kevin McNamara lodged an early day motion in Parliament calling for a public inquiry, and, almost immediately, more than 100 other MPs backed his demands. It didn't come as a great surprise given the enormous pressure now on the Army, one of Britain's greatest institutions.

The public was also extremely supportive after the launch of our campaign, and we got many letters, some of them from other families who had loved ones in the

Army. A handful even included some money to help us out, for expenses such as train fares from Perth to London, and it touched us deeply.

By now the juggernaut was gathering pace, and there were developments on a near daily basis. On 4 July 2002, for example, the House of Commons Defence Select Committee announced it was going to hold its own investigation into the Deepcut deaths once the police probe was over. A day later, Surrey Police announced it was extending the remit of its own inquiry and would now also examine the cases of Sean Benton and Cheryl James. It was all happening fast.

Out of the blue, the Army revealed it had destroyed three of the four uniforms worn by the soldiers on the nights they died, as well as some of the documentation relating to the guns. It came as quite a shock and probably only emerged because Surrey Police was now asking questions about the four deaths. We were told James's uniform was not one of those disposed of, and, as far as I am aware, the Army still has it today. However, we are not entitled to it because it is 'Ministry of Defence property'. In any case, very little of it remains after it was cut into small pieces during belated forensic tests, but that's not the point. To my mind, the Army had no right to burn the other uniforms without the permission of the families.

Sordid accounts of what life was like within Deepcut started to emerge over the summer of 2002, with newspapers and TV news programmes carrying frequent allegations about soldiers being bullied or sexually abused. On 24 July 2002, one former soldier gave an interview to Channel 4 News claiming that Sean Benton, who had been his friend, was tormented by his superiors in the days leading up to his death. Trevor Hunter said he saw Private Benton being punched by members of staff while exercising, punished for saying he did not like football and subjected to verbal abuse on a daily basis. He also alleged that one senior non-commissioned officer (NCO) had tried to 'break' his friend because his 'face didn't fit'. In a separate interview, a former corporal also claimed senior officers blocked her attempts to report Private Benton being thrown out of a second-floor window. It was horrific stuff.

Three days later, on 27 July 2002, another female former recruit told the *Daily Mirror* she had been 'terrorised' by a lesbian officer during her time at Deepcut and claimed she was subjected to a 'merciless campaign of bullying, abuse and physical punishment'. Emma Watson, who started at the barracks as a 19-year-old in 1994, said that within hours of arriving at the camp she was 'beasted' – humiliated – by one officer, then forced to drill on her own at 10 p.m. On another occasion she said she was ordered to do what was called the 'Grand National', which entailed running along the length of the firing line wearing 45 lb of kit until she dropped from exhaustion.

It was during this time that speculation mounted that Cheryl James had been sexually harassed by officers during her final days at the camp. However, I still wasn't sure how relevant any of this was to James, since he had only been at Deepcut for six weeks before he died, and he'd seemed to get on with everyone as far as we could see. Certainly, he had never mentioned any issues at the barracks, and if all of this bullying and sexual intimidation was going on around him, it seemed he must have been totally oblivious to it. Then again, there was always the terrifying thought in the back of my mind that he had become mixed up with it on the very night he died. This fear was compounded when, on 4 August 2002, the *Sunday Express* ran a story that speculated James might have been killed after rejecting homosexual advances at the barracks. The article said detectives were looking at that as one possible explanation, and claimed that Deepcut was becoming synonymous with sex and violence.

Bullying in the Army was becoming a hot topic in the news, and in September 2002 another family came forward to claim their 19-year-old son may have been killed during his time with the Royal Logistic Corps. Jim and Barbara Little told BBC News they had never been convinced by accounts that their boy, Dale, shot himself in the early hours of 22 July 1995, while serving in Bosnia. They pointed to the fact he had written to his girlfriend shortly before his death saying how much he was looking forward to returning to England to see her and his young son, Jordan. Like us, the Littles were given little information about the tragedy, and there was no proper investigation into Dale's death because the Army concluded he had shot himself. One bullet, one body, draw your own conclusion. The Littles came forward to back our demands for a public inquiry, but they quickly faded into the background, with the attention firmly on the Deepcut Four.

Another mother who came forward was Jenny Shipley, whose son, David, was found dead in unusual circumstances in Germany, again while serving with the Royal Logistic Corps. Aged 20, he was found drowned in a paddling pool on 22 June 2002, at the end of a gala day at the Bielefeld barracks to mark the Queen's Golden Jubilee. What made David's case more intriguing was the fact he had served alongside my James at Deepcut and had reported for guard duty on the very night James died. He was one of the many soldiers eventually interviewed by Surrey Police about the shooting before being posted to Germany, only to be found face down in a pool fewer than three days later.

Deepcut was beginning to sound like the camp from hell, an Army barracks out of control. The media reports only added to our belief that something sinister had been going on during the time our children died. As horrified as we all were, little did we know the worst was still to come.

As summer turned to autumn, Jim and I still had more questions than answers. No one had yet come back to us with any concrete theories on what might have happened, and there seemed to have been no major developments as far as the police investigation was concerned. Despite asking numerous times, we also had no explanation as to why James had scratches on his hands and marks on his neck, or why he had black eyes and a swollen nose. Any time we asked the investigating officers, they would shrug their shoulders and simply say, 'We don't know. It was never checked.' The problem was that the post-mortem carried out on James had been extremely basic and simply involved his being opened up and his organs weighed. That was it. Surrey Police did apologise for the inadequacy of the examination and admitted that, with hindsight, the post-mortem should have been done better. They had messed up and they acknowledged it, but they said it was too late to do anything about it now.

Jim and I thought differently, however, and in late September 2002 we toyed with the idea of doing what many people would consider unthinkable and ask for a second post-mortem to take place. Certainly, we had nothing to lose, because we had already lost our son and nothing was ever going to bring him back. With that in mind, there was only one thing to do: we had to have James exhumed.

11. Breakthrough

No parent should be forced into the indignity of exhuming a child. It's such an inhuman concept. Yet that is exactly what Jim and I faced as we awoke on the cold and misty morning of 2 October 2002. We had agonised over whether it was the right thing to do and what people would think about us, and I really felt for James. He had only been buried six months earlier and should have been resting in peace, but here he was about to be dug up and pulled apart again at our behest. By the same token, while it would be one day of trauma for us, we knew it could lead to a lifetime of having answers about what had happened to our son.

When it came to making the final decision, we didn't feel we had much choice. Jim and I weren't happy with the way James's post-mortem had been carried out in March, and if there was evidence on our son's body to indicate why he had died then we needed to get to it. Crucially, we wanted to find out whether or not there was anything under James's fingernails – such as mud or traces of someone else's skin – that might indicate a struggle had taken place, and if there was any gunpowder residue on his hands to show whether or not he had pulled the trigger of the gun himself. The bruising on James's face, and the scratches and marks on his hands and neck, also warranted further investigation, in our opinion.

Had these simple examinations been carried out during the original post-mortem, the chances are we would already have a clear idea of what had happened to James on the night he died, yet, inexplicably, they weren't. It seemed to us that having been informed a soldier had shot himself, the coroner had simply gone through the motions without looking for anything out of the ordinary. Jim and I were quite bitter about this, because we were now faced with having to dig up our dead son six months later in order to find the answers for ourselves.

James was exhumed shortly before dawn, although the operation to prepare the plot started hours earlier in total darkness. Photographers and journalists had camped out from midnight in a bid to get a prime spot for the dig starting. By first light, a handful had clambered onto the perimeter wall, while others had moved to higher land to get a view down into the open grave. It didn't take the police long to move the photographers to lower ground after it emerged they were seeing more than they ought to: James's coffin had actually collapsed under the weight of the earth and he had to be placed into another casket before being lifted out of the ground. It wasn't a picture anyone wanted appearing in the TV bulletins or the morning papers.

Wellshill Cemetery was only a couple of miles from our house on Colonsay Street, and normally it was a place I liked going to. It was pretty, and I loved the peace and tranquillity of being there as I remembered all the good times we'd had with James. But on the morning of 2 October 2002, it was the last place on Earth I wanted to be, so we didn't attend. I tried to put the exhumation out of my mind and pretend it wasn't happening, and I really did not want to think too much about what state James's body would be in, but it was tough and I kept conjuring up horrid pictures in my mind. From the very moment I

I was only about five or six when this photo was taken, so it dates back to when the abuse from Uncle George started. I'm standing outside the flat my mother and I stayed in with my grandmother, not long after I sparked a police search by wandering off with my dolly.

Aged six, I was visiting some relatives when this photograph was taken.

A rare photo of Uncle George in his younger days when he was serving in the Royal Navy. It was taken long before I was born, probably during his time in Hong Kong.

This is me and Uncle George, lazing about in his garden. I was roughly ten years old when this was taken during one of the many weekends I spent there at that time.

I was so happy to become Mrs Collinson the day I married Jim. We're standing on the banks of the River Tay on what turned out to be a glorious summer's afternoon.

Jim and I pose with baby James at the Hogmanay party on 31 December 1984. Only a few hours earlier we'd had a scare when Jim dropped James at the top of the stairs.

James was only about three when this was taken in our flat on Dunsinane Drive in Perth. He looked so cheeky and happy, and he was.

A rare family outing to Blackpool. I have fond memories of that trip, even if it was to the same town Uncle George took me to on holiday.

James and Stuart were inseparable as little boys. In this picture they are doing one of their favourite things: eating. James, in particular, loved his food, but he was so energetic he burned it off quickly.

James was so excited about setting off for his first day at school. All the attention was on James, but, being competitive, Stuart insisted on being bigger than his brother and asked to stand on a bucket!

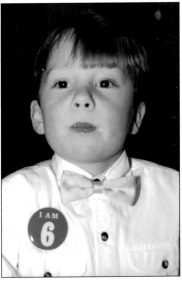

James's sixth birthday party was held at Auntie Betty's house. I was pregnant with Claire at this time, so my aunt offered to help out. Doesn't James look so smart in his silver bow tie?

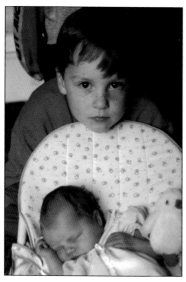

James was proud as punch the day we brought baby Claire home from hospital. He was six years old and very protective of his little sister.

James's final school photograph was taken at Perth High School when he was 16. It wouldn't be long before he was off to the Army.

Posing with Claire and Stuart, James looked resplendent in his uniform the day he passed out, at the second time of asking. I'll always remember that day at Pirbright as one of the happiest of my life.

This is one of the few images we have of James in his uniform.
We have no idea whose dog it is.

Surrounded by green fields and trees, I liked the look of the Princess Royal Barracks – at least from the outside. In many ways, I thought it looked like a university or college campus.

The four Deepcut soldiers (clockwise from top left): James Collinson, Cheryl James, Geoff Gray and Sean Benton. (Courtesy of the *Scottish Sunday Express*)

One of the many floral arrangements on the day of James's funeral. We placed it at the top of his grave to symbolise his pillow. In our minds, it made it easier to think of his resting place like a bed.

Jim and I take great comfort from visiting James's grave in Perth. I take great pride in arranging his flowers just so, but I always ensure I tend to them from the back of the headstone. I can't face reading my son's name.
(© Graeme Hunter Photography)

The front page of the *Scottish Sunday Express* on the day the newspaper launched its Justice For James campaign. (Courtesy of the *Scottish Sunday Express*)

Malcolm and I tied the knot in a low-key ceremony at Gretna Registry Office. We wanted a quiet wedding surrounded by only a handful of friends. It was a perfect day.

Frank Swann promised us so much but delivered so little when he offered to help us solve the Deepcut mystery for £1. He is pictured in his caravan, which doubled as a supposed laboratory.
(Courtesy of the *Scottish Sunday Express*)

When my father came back into my life in 2004 after an absence of more than 30 years, I learned I had family I'd never known. Dad is in the middle, and I am standing next to my brother James.

opened my eyes in the morning, all I could think about was my poor James.

Jim, Stuart, Claire and I jumped in the car and drove out of Perth to escape as best we could. We were determined to try to have as normal a day as possible in nearby Dundee, and the plan was to have some nice family time away from the media and to treat Stuart and Claire as much as we could. However, everywhere we turned we found reminders of the exhumation. When we turned on the car radio it was the top story on the local news, and when we went out for lunch it was being talked about on Sky News on the television in the corner of the restaurant. It seemed there was no way to avoid what was happening to our James.

In the afternoon we went bowling and shopping, but there was a terrible tension in the air between the four of us, and as much as we tried to make it an enjoyable outing, it was impossible. I couldn't fully concentrate; James was uppermost in my mind wherever we went. I ended up clock-watching, trying to work out where his body would have been at any given time and what would be taking place next. It was a catch-22 situation for me because while I was trying to block out events at the cemetery, at the same time I desperately wanted to know what was going on and if there had been any developments. The irony was that we fled to Dundee to escape but that was exactly where James was being taken to for the second post-mortem, and it's likely that we were only ever a mile or two from him. At least we weren't so well known by the people of Dundee as we were by people in Perth, so we could escape the sympathetic looks.

The fresh examination took place at the new Tayside Police mortuary in Dundee and was carried out by a Home Office pathologist on behalf of Surrey Police. Our legal team had also employed an independent expert – a man who was a senior lecturer in forensic pathology at Glasgow University – to be present and to observe the proceedings. We had requested that a few specific things be carried out, including that James's head be X-rayed to confirm whether or not his nose was broken, that his fingernails be checked for signs of a struggle, and his hands tested for any gunpowder residue.

James's body was returned to his grave at about 6 p.m. and, again, we chose not to be present. Both Surrey Police and the Army had offered to pay for another full military funeral when he was reinterred, but there was no way we could have endured that. To have stood by and watched our son being buried once was bad enough, but twice? That would have been too much to bear. Instead, only five people were present as James was laid to rest again: our two police liaison officers, two investigating officers from Surrey Police and a minister, who made a short blessing. During the original funeral in April, Jim, Stuart, Claire and I all placed a long-stemmed rose on top of James's coffin. We asked our family liaison officers to do the same for us at the second interment, since we weren't there, and they duly obliged.

When the liaison officers came back to the house after the reinterment, I was surprised to see that they were in funeral attire. I thought it was very respectful, and it really strengthened the bond that was developing between us. They were good people. However, they barely had time to sit down before we were firing questions at them. Did the pathologist do this? Did he do that? Did he find anything? And so on. The officers were quite hesitant, because they didn't want to upset us with the grim nature of the findings, but we pushed them. We were desperate for even the smallest nugget of information that might offer us hope and justify what we had done to James. I asked, in particular, about whether an X-ray had been carried out because I was convinced James's nose was broken, such was the swelling in his face. The answer made us flinch. 'There was no need for an X-ray,' one of the pair said slowly. 'Unfortunately James's skull fell in when they went to move it. The whole area was shattered.'

The officers went on to tell us that there had been no opportunity to examine under James's nails either: they had fallen off. It was traumatic to hear and a bit deflating. Jim and I tried to stay positive, however, because many of the new forensic test results had yet to be confirmed. When the officers left, I felt an overwhelming sense of relief that our ordeal was over and that a post-mortem – a proper post-mortem – had been done, and on our terms. I felt as if that day had dragged on for ever.

Later that evening, once everything had quietened down and the last of the lingering photographers had disappeared, we all went to the cemetery. It was an upsetting experience for us because James's grave had the look of a new plot again, reminding us about what had happened at dawn. We laid some flowers and had a few quiet moments to ourselves. I consoled myself with the knowledge that we could now arrange for a headstone to be put in place, and at last James could rest in peace: he would never be disturbed again.

I always feel comforted visiting James's grave, although I still can't face the headstone or read his name on the front. Normally I walk to the back and tend to any flowers from behind: it's just too painful for me to do anything else. I also choose not to talk to him. Some people like talking to the dead, but not me. Jim is one of those people and it upsets me. The way he speaks to the grave, it's as if James is still really there – it's clearly something that gives him comfort – but I find it hard to watch. James will always be in my heart, but I can't bring myself to associate him with the person that is under the ground. I don't know what Jim said to him when we went back to the cemetery after the reinterment, but I imagine he said, 'Sorry, son.' Stuart did what he often does during his visits to the grave: he took James a can of beer and left it there. 'You'll need that,' he said. It's little wonder.

That day was one of the hardest in my life, almost as hard as the day we buried James first time around. Even now I find 2 October every year is a struggle, and wherever I am, and whatever I am doing, my thoughts are only of James. We went through a lot during the course of that day, but in our heart of hearts we knew that it would be worth it. Two months would pass before we would be proved right.

I had been back in Perth for about six months by now, and Malcolm was missing me terribly. He had been 100 per cent behind my decision to head to Scotland, even though he knew I might never return to him. To be fair, I hadn't gone back to Perth to be with Jim as husband and wife, and rekindle my old life in the family home: we had gone too far for that. Instead, I was there only for James, Stuart and Claire, and I had been staying most of the time with my mum, who had returned to Scotland after separating from my stepfather. If truth be told, I felt a bit of a nomad, because I would spend some nights on the couch at her house, some nights on the recliner chair at Auntie Betty's house, and the odd night at Jim's whenever I was needed there for the kids or for the campaign. It was a case of wherever I laid my hat, that was my home.

Malcolm and I stayed in constant contact when I was in Perth, either by phone or by old-fashioned post, and we kept the romance alive from afar, but I dearly wanted us to be together again. Eventually the council found me a tiny two-bedroom flat, and Malcolm and the boys moved north from Reading to be with me in Scotland permanently.

I had been so focused on the campaign and on finding out what had happened to James that it was great seeing them again after all that time. When you lose a child, part of you dies with them, and I felt that strongly. I had become a different person in the six months I had been back in Perth, but Malcolm had waited patiently for me. Somehow, despite being bottom of my priorities and having been pushed aside, he had managed to put up with it. He was my rock.

Life became slightly more complicated after that, and I found myself playing mother in two different households. In the morning, Jim would come to my new flat and drive me to Colonsay Street, where I would get Claire ready for school before tidying the house and doing the washing and ironing. I would finish at about lunchtime and then head home to my own place to catch up on the housework before returning to Jim's for Claire coming in from school. I made her dinner and stayed with her until Jim got home from work, then it was off back to the other side of Perth to do it all again. All this was on top of trying to campaign for a public inquiry. It was a strange arrangement and I don't quite know how I managed, but I did.

Our campaign was given a major boost the week after the exhumation when the *Scottish Sunday Express* launched a 'Justice for James' crusade to lobby for a public inquiry. I remember walking past the news-stands that Sunday morning and screaming out from the front page were the words 'GIVE US JUSTICE FOR JAMES'. It was fantastic, and it filled me with emotion. I scrambled around in my purse for the coins I needed to buy the paper, with tears streaming down my face, as the newsagent smiled knowingly at me. Inside was a two-page spread featuring a petition voucher for members of the public to fill in to send to the newspaper offices. The coupons would then be collated and sent on to 10 Downing Street. Although the media had been a working tool for us and we knew they were on our side, this was the first time that someone had decided to campaign on our behalf as well as encourage the public to do the same.

The coverage really helped spur us on, and within the first week, hundreds of people had sent in their vouchers to the *Sunday Express* offices in Glasgow. After that, any time we walked down the street in Perth we would have strangers coming up to us and telling us we had their support, while letters started arriving at Jim's house addressed simply to 'The Collinsons, Perth, Scotland'.

Other newspapers continued to take an interest in Deepcut and further revelations emerged about what life was like inside the camp. In fact, the more sordid stories that came out, the more the media picked up on the scandal; the more that newspapers covered Deepcut, the more new sordid stories came out. It was a vicious circle of good news as far as we were concerned.

Throughout October and November, the *Sunday Express* was at the forefront of the coverage: it had to be because it had launched such a high-profile campaign. On 20 October 2002, the newspaper revealed that the bullying regime at the Princess Royal Barracks dated back more than 20 years, with an article featuring an anonymous female private who claimed that when she was at the camp, as a 20-year-old in 1982, recruits were threatened with fictitious charges if they refused the advances of officers. The higher the ranking, the easier it was for a private to be taken advantage of, she said. Another woman alleged she had been raped by a married sergeant, but when she went to complain she was put under so much pressure by male officers she retracted her statement. The same story told how 45 recruits had gone absent without leave (AWOL) from Deepcut in the space of just two years, with one mother claiming her son refused to go back because he feared the 'gay guards'.

So much was coming out about Deepcut that there came a point at which we were no longer surprised or shocked by the catalogue of alleged abuse. It all merged into one big horror story and made us feel even worse about the fact we had allowed our boy to join the Army. It got to the stage that I honestly didn't want to hear any more. We couldn't help but think, 'What the hell was James being forced to put up with before he died?'

It was at about this time that a man called Frank Swann came into our lives. He was a forensics and ballistics expert, and he had been working with the BBC on another *Frontline Scotland* documentary about the deaths at Deepcut. The programme-makers put us in touch with him, and he offered to work on behalf of the families to uncover any evidence that the Army and the police might have missed. His fee would be just £1, and he promised he would use his knowledge and expertise to find us some answers. It was an incredible gesture, and Jim and I were in tears after we spoke with him on the telephone. We couldn't believe someone had volunteered to help us. It seemed too good to be true, but more of that to come later.

With the sheer number of allegations emerging from Deepcut, Surrey Police began to issue ever more frequent press releases to update the media on the progress of its investigation. There was a great deal of pressure on the force from newspapers, never mind from the four families. Officials triumphantly announced that they had 30 officers working on the cases and that they had spoken to more than 500 people, that they had been to Germany, and that they had facilitated the second post-mortem on James. To the outside world, it probably looked like Surrey Police was doing a good job, but we were starting to feel they were doing nothing except covering their tracks. All of this so-called investigative work should have been carried out in March, not October. It was too little, too late, and a mere publicity exercise, as far as the families were concerned.

Behind the scenes, the fact was that Surrey Police was struggling to cope with the scale and complexity of the four Deepcut inquiries, particularly because the same officers had to deal with the case of 13-year-old schoolgirl Milly Dowler, whose body had been discovered on 18 September 2002.

We also found out that senior police officers had been holding secret meetings with the Army about the Deepcut case without telling any of the families. We wondered why they would have to do such a thing. What did they have to discuss with the top brass at the barracks that they didn't say to us? I was dumbfounded, because as far as I was concerned the Army was the enemy. It seemed farcical and only added to my initial feelings about the truth behind James's death being covered up, and it made me question Surrey Police's commitment to finding out what happened. After all, it was me who had asked for a second post-mortem; it was me who then had to make suggestions to the pathologist about what to look for during the examination. I was beginning to feel like I had to spoon-feed the police, and Jim and I were rapidly losing faith in the force. As things stood, Surrey Police just didn't look capable of finding the answers about James's death that we so desperately craved.

Towards the end of the year, Surrey Police summoned Jim and Geoff to a meeting at which they were told the cap badge belonging to James had been found. It came as a surprise to us, because we never knew the gold-coloured badge that had been clipped to his beret was even missing. Then we felt anger. For months we had been asking, without success, for the police to carry out a fingertip search of the area where James had died. Incredibly, no search had ever been carried out at the scene or around the nearby perimeter fence, either by the Army or the police. Eventually when they caved in to our demands they found the cap badge. It was now 10 December 2002. It was a scandal. Once more we felt that we were telling the police how to do their own jobs.

The situation was worse for Geoff and Diane Gray, because, as well as James's badge, the sweep of the area had found part of their son's skull. It had been lying there for more than a year and showed just how incompetent Surrey Police were. Indeed, we believe that they still wouldn't have found the cap badge and skull piece to this day had we not bullied them into doing the search.

The honest, if amusing, truth of it all is that I had repeatedly asked for the fingertip search as a result of having gone to a spiritualist, who had told me, 'The evidence is in the undergrowth.' It didn't make sense to me at the time, but we told the family liaison officers anyway. When you're desperate for a breakthrough, you'll try every possible avenue, and this was a lead of sorts, even if it did come from an unexpected source. It turned out to be true: Jim was told by Surrey Police that the cap badge had been discovered in the undergrowth not far from James's body but a few yards outside the barracks, on the other side of the perimeter fence.

Despite the incompetence, we took the discovery as a possible turning point in the investigation. As far as I was concerned, a cap badge, to a soldier, was something to be worn with pride and honour. It signified their alliance to a regiment and there was no way James would have thrown it away. We felt most likely it had been pulled off by someone during a scuffle. The fact was it hadn't just fallen off or been unclipped; it had been torn off the beret, and part of the ripped material from the cap was actually still attached to it.

Our view that James had been involved in a fight before his death was strengthened because of another BBC documentary that had been broadcast a week earlier, which gave the most conclusive evidence to date that Deepcut was out of control. The *Panorama* 'Bullied to Death' programme said the barracks was dominated by fear, violence and sexual harassment, named some of the alleged worst offending officers, and speculated that a killer might be on the loose. It told of young soldiers being punched and kicked, or forced to carry out humiliating sexual acts. For the first time, a number of former recruits also went public on camera to tell about their own ordeals, with many saying that it was impossible to report instances of bullying because the officer you would have to report it to was the same person you would be complaining about.

We had worked with the *Panorama* team for months in the lead-up to the broadcast, but it still made difficult viewing, particularly for the families of Sean Benton and Cheryl James. One of Private Benton's friends told how he had seen Sean being regularly bullied and seriously assaulted, while Private James was often seen crying.

Private Benton's friend Trevor Hunter – who had already spoken out in a previous television interview – told the documentary about a particularly nasty beating that Sean had endured at the hands of a sergeant. He said, 'He was in his room sleeping at night and a group of people came into his room and they were wearing the standard S1 respirator that we all wear in chemical training. It basically covers the outline of your features so nobody can see you. They proceeded to beat him up in his bed, to his obvious injury. He had considerable bruising through his body.'

Lance Corporal Terri Lewis told *Panorama* that Sean went to the guardroom to report having been thrown out of a second-floor window one night, only to be told to 'ignore it'. She said, 'The incidents in terms of when he was getting beaten in bed or other incidents in front of the parade just had to be ignored. It was part and parcel of his initiation within the Army.'

The same lance corporal had also encountered Cheryl James during her time at Deepcut and told the BBC of seeing her in tears. She said, 'I was aware that a certain sergeant took an extreme strong liking to Cheryl and made her life hell. I heard of an incident . . . in which he made her go to the squadron office on her own and a conversation took place. The discussion went towards sex. Cheryl turned round and said, "I'm in a relationship. I don't want to be involved; I don't want any of this." Obviously the sergeant, to be knocked back – how dare she knock back a sergeant. It visibly shook the girl up, and not long after, she took her life.'

When I watched the programme, I thought back to what James had told me about the night he was kicked down a muddy embankment by a sergeant. James said at the time he was fine with it, as he had expected discipline, yet I was now wondering whether he had actually been subjected to the kind of bullying behaviour highlighted in the media but was one of the recruits who simply accepted it as part of everyday Army life. That said, I still was of the mind that I didn't want to hear too much about this side of Deepcut, because it scared me to think of James being a target when I hadn't been able to help and protect him.

The *Panorama* programme was powerful stuff and opened up a new can of worms surrounding Deepcut and the British Army in general, and it bolstered my belief that the announcement of a public inquiry into the four deaths would soon become a mere formality. Too much was emerging about the camp by the end of 2002 to simply ignore it, and with the continual media pressure and public opinion behind us we genuinely felt an announcement by the Labour government would be imminent. What's more, the Armed Forces Minister Adam Ingram had also just granted permission for our independent ballistics expert Frank Swann to go inside Deepcut and carry out tests.

Things were getting better and better, and days later we got the breakthrough we so desperately needed when we finally learned the results of the second post-mortem. They showed there was no gunpowder residue on James's hands – which would have proved he pulled the trigger himself – and indicated that there were indentations on his right knuckle, suggesting that the gun had actually been placed into his hand after his death. The few crime-scene photographs we had seen up until this point showed James was found with his finger over the trigger of the gun, which lay across the top of his body, but now we had evidence to suggest it had been forced into position. I tried to stay calm, but my mind was racing with all the possibilities.

The post-mortem also showed James's jaw had been fractured, and there was no explanation for this, because the bullet entry wound in his chin had been in soft tissue and not through bone. This suggested his jaw was perhaps broken before the shooting – again backing up our belief that James had been in a fight.

I was excited by the post-mortem results, because I knew they would open up new avenues for us and could help to force a public inquiry. However, part of me felt sad, because deep down I still wanted someone to prove that James had chosen to take his own life, that it was his decision to leave this world, but these results showed the opposite. I was now tormented by what my boy might have gone through in those last few moments.

The first Christmas without James was a difficult time for us all. We discussed as a family what we should do and decided we should try to have as normal a time as possible, particularly because Claire was still only 11. We put up a tree, we bought presents for one another, and we had the full Christmas dinner planned. Jim and I spoiled Stuart and Claire that year and bought them everything they wanted. We went a bit overboard, if truth be told, and I think we wanted to make up for the year they'd had and try to compensate them for the loss of their brother as well as for the lack of time we had spent with them. Yet it just wasn't the same without James, and we simply went through the motions.

I stayed overnight at Jim's house on Christmas Eve, but there was no excitement as we went to open our presents in the morning. Where there used to be laughter around the tree, there were only tears. While in the past the living room would be covered in wrapping paper as parcels were torn open within seconds, this time around we had to force ourselves to even pick them up. We might as well have not bothered.

We all got in the car and drove round to my flat, where Malcolm and the boys were waiting patiently to open their presents. I had hoped their excitement would rub off on us and bring out the festive feeling, but my heart was still very heavy.

By the time Boxing Day arrived, I was champing at the bit to get back to campaigning. I wanted the phone to be ringing and for journalists to be coming to ask us questions about the latest developments, but, of course, it was quiet. Jim and I spent the remainder of the Christmas period catching up on paperwork and looking at ways to take the campaign forward and start afresh after the New Year. We weren't alone. The other families were in the same position and hadn't really celebrated Christmas either.

I spent Hogmanay in the flat with Malcolm but it too was a non-event. I went to bed long before the bells rang out to signal the start of 2003. It had been a whirlwind nine months and my life had been blown apart by James's death, and I didn't particularly want to sit and reflect on it all as midnight arrived. I had changed in so many ways – we all had. All I could think about as I drifted off to sleep was how tough 2002 had been. It should have been the year we celebrated our eldest son turning 18, but instead we had laid flowers on his grave on his birthday. Thank God the year was over.

12. The So-called Expert

I will never forget the first time I met Frank Swann, the man who confidently predicted he was going to tell me how my James died and in doing so blow the lid on a series of Army cover-ups and solve the mystery of Deepcut in one fell swoop. It was the early autumn of 2002, and having already spoken to him on the phone a number of times, I had expected someone sophisticated and coiffured and most probably wearing a designer suit, or at the very least a shirt and tie.

What was waiting for us in the lobby of a hotel in Surrey was someone completely different, to say the least. I can only describe Frank Swann as an odd-looking character, a big hulk of a man who was in his mid-to-late 50s and was wearing casual trousers, a sweatshirt and more jewellery than I had ever seen on a person before. He had rings on almost every finger, while on his wrist were lots of jangling bracelets, one of which had tiny guns hanging from it. Frank also had dyed-black hair and Teddy-boy-style sideburns that, to me, signified a man who didn't want to grow old gracefully. He was also carrying a replica SA-80 rifle. Put it this way, he was a world away from the lawyers, QCs, barristers, senior police officers and Army officials we were used to dealing with on a day-to-day basis.

It was Jane MacSorley, a producer for the BBC, who

had put us in touch with Frank a few weeks earlier, after she had hired him for a *Frontline Scotland* investigation that was to be aired in October. She said he had 40 years' experience in forensic science and that he was convinced the Deepcut deaths were not self-inflicted, and she thought he might be a major help to our campaign. When I spoke to Frank on the telephone, he came across as someone who was well versed in the field and he seemed to know everything about James's death. He also said he was more than happy to put all his other cases to one side and investigate the four Deepcut deaths – but only if we employed him to do so.

It has been well documented in the media that the families hired Frank Swann for just £1, but there is more to the story than we have ever revealed. Yes, he was keen to help, but not for free and, to begin with, certainly not for £1. Instead, Frank Swann told us he wanted to be well paid for working on the Deepcut cases. After all, he was going to be taking a long time away from his other work to concentrate on the four soldiers. We were desperate for him to look into the deaths and asked him how much he would charge us for doing it. '£10,000 per family,' Frank said, matter-of-factly, during our first telephone call. I flinched. We didn't have that kind of money; I don't think any of the families did. I hadn't been back at work since James had died and our finances were extremely tight. There was no way we could afford this. There was an awkward pause.

'OK, all right then. How about I do it for £1 per family instead then?' Frank asked. It was quite a drop in price, to say the least, and we didn't have to be asked twice, but you have to wonder if he had really expected us to pay him £40,000 for the job.

We put the money issue to the back of our minds, and in the weeks that followed, Jim and I had a number of phone calls with Frank during which he spoke of his determination for justice to be done. He said all the right things and told us about his own grandfather, who had been in the Army, and insisted he had great respect for Britain's servicemen and women. Frank also claimed he wanted to solve the four deaths as much for other British soldiers as the Deepcut families, and said he was applying for permission to carry out tests within the barracks. It was all music to our ears.

Jane MacSorley had asked Frank to carry out ballistics tests at a firing range in Surrey for the *Frontline Scotland* programme and suggested that it would be a good opportunity for us to meet him for the first time. However, we felt slightly uneasy about being anywhere that live guns would be tested, so we shied away from that and arranged to meet him and the TV crew at a hotel later.

When the time came, Frank sauntered in carrying a replica SA-80 rifle inside a carry case. It wasn't real – it was made of plastic, but looked pretty real to me – and he wanted to bring it out to show us how it worked. That would have been fine had we not been sitting in the lobby, with hotel guests and other members of the public looking on. It wasn't Frank's brightest idea, and it didn't exactly leave us with the best first impression of our new 'expert'.

We all left the hotel and instead headed to the nearby home of one of the BBC cameramen, where Frank eventually did get the replica gun out and explain its inner workings. He really seemed to know what he was talking about, detailing how many rounds per second the SA-80 can fire and what the kickback was like and so on. I didn't know anything about guns, and I was impressed by Frank's knowledge.

With his abundance of jewellery, Frank clinked every time he moved, so much so that he was eventually asked to take the bracelets off because they were interfering with the sound quality on the TV recording. He refused. It was our first glimpse of the arrogant streak he would show more than once over the next few years.

I didn't hold any of Frank's oddities against him in the beginning, however. If anything, his unusual appearance and his gruff ways only enhanced the feeling I had that he would get answers for us. Many of the world's best minds tend to be slightly eccentric, and Frank certainly fitted that mould. I also found him witty and intelligent. All in all, we had faith in him and we were grateful that, at long last, we had an expert on our side who appeared to know what he was talking about. What's more, he was telling us what some of us wanted to hear: that our children had not killed themselves and that he could, and would, prove it. In James's case, he spoke about how he believed the pattern of blood splatter wasn't consistent with a self-inflicted wound and claimed the position of the rifle also showed James couldn't have killed himself. Having viewed the scenes of crime photographs, Frank also insisted the gunpowder tattooing on James's chin was consistent with a third party having been involved.

I was captivated every time Frank Swann spoke about Deepcut and outlined why he thought the Army was wrong in saying my James had taken his own life. When Frank gave a newspaper interview to reveal that the Deepcut families had employed him, he promised to 'apply scientific protocol and methodology using every forensic method available, including ultraviolet reconstruction'. He sounded so convincing. Frank Swann was our ray of light, and I truly believed he would make sure a public inquiry was an inevitability.

Shortly after that first meeting, Frank posted a note on our Justice for James website attacking the Surrey Police investigation and claiming the force was 'as good as a chocolate cup of tea'. He was enjoying the publicity he suddenly attracted, and he loved playing cat and mouse with the police, as if trying to get one up on them all the time. Anything the detectives announced he dismissed immediately, such was his sense of self-importance. He had no respect for them at all, and we noticed it was beginning to hinder the relationship we had with the officers. All through our campaign, the families had an unwritten rule that we had to remain dignified, and no matter what we might have felt about the Army or Surrey Police, we had to keep it to ourselves. Not Frank, though. He had other ideas.

Frank wasn't shy in making sure his point, and only his point, was put across. He was so full of himself at times and very dismissive of anyone else's opinion, no matter who they were. He would argue that black was, in fact, white, if he truly felt it. That said, he was very convincing and appeared to have great confidence that his theories were 100 per cent accurate, so, at least to begin with, we didn't doubt him. For instance, before he had even stepped inside the barracks to carry out tests, he announced to the world that there was a 'high probability' of establishing the causes of death in three of the cases and that he was '70 per cent certain' that James had not killed himself. He was some man, and the media lapped it up just as much as we did.

We didn't have many meetings with Frank, and almost all of our communication was done via telephone or email. The second time we met him face to face was ahead of a special *Tonight with Trevor McDonald* programme for ITV due to be broadcast on 4 November 2002. We gathered at one of London's top hotels, and while it was probably the swankiest place I had ever been in my life, Frank complained about everything. The restaurant menu wasn't good enough and the standard of food wasn't good enough, and so on for the whole night. Boy, he was hard work, I thought to myself.

In another posting on the Justice for James website, Frank said he had a reputation for 'telling it as it is'. He sure did, but he also seemed to have this strange attitude that everyone, no matter who they were, from the police to the hotel chef, was against him. It was beginning to grate on me.

To be fair, I didn't know very much about Frank, and he gave little away as far as his personal background was concerned. He told us about the 'vast number' of investigations he had been involved in over the years, and said he had previously been employed by Surrey Police to assist in some of their cases. He sounded extremely experienced and, in our eyes, was a great asset to us, no matter what his personality was like.

However, we did receive an alarming email from someone who claimed he used to work with Frank some years ago. The man described him as a 'Walter Mitty character' who used to drive a car mocked up on the inside to look like a police car. The same email questioned to what extent our ballistics expert had any expertise in the field whatsoever, and informed us that Frank had spent time working as a removal man. It was worrying stuff, but we were so captivated by what Frank was telling us about Deepcut that we simply ignored the warning. In fact, I actually thought the man was another member of the Establishment deliberately trying to put us off so that we would never find out the truth about what happened to our loved ones. We just didn't want to believe Frank wasn't the man he said he was. I did mention the email to Frank, and he confirmed that he knew the sender but said the pair had never seen eye to eye and put it down to a grudge. 'Fair enough,' I thought, but the seeds of doubt had been planted.

Frank rolled up to Deepcut on the morning of 13 January 2003, to be met by a posse of reporters, photographers and camera crews. I had been dreading that day coming, because, as much as I hoped the visit would provide some answers, I knew the final moments of my son's life were about to be reconstructed. I really couldn't face the thought of Frank firing a gun at a mannequin posing as James, as he planned to do on the first day.

Frank rarely missed an opportunity for a sound bite, and it was no different that morning when he saw the assembled media waiting for his arrival. According to the *Daily Mail* report the next day, Frank said, 'I'm hoping we will find out the truth by conducting a number of tests using laser, ultra-violet, reconstruction and detection equipment and by comparing the statements of the people concerned.

'At the moment I have personal views on two of the deaths who were in my view not self-inflicted, a third who we feel 70 per cent sure was not self-inflicted and a fourth who we do not know.'

It was typical Frank, but this is where it all started going wrong. His scientific laboratory, for instance, turned out to be nothing more than a run-down caravan. I couldn't believe my eyes when I saw it being towed through the gates of the Princess Royal Barracks.

Frank said he planned to investigate the four deaths individually, starting with James, since his was the most recent shooting. He was going to visit the scene, talk to eyewitnesses, carry out tests on firearms both at the perimeter fence where James was found and on the rifle range, and use lasers to plot the trajectory of the bullet. The investigation sounded comprehensive. However, looking back on it now, I'm not sure he did anything more useful than drink cups of tea and sit about a lot.

When he was inside the barracks, we had expected to be kept informed about what he was doing. We heard nothing. Indeed, the only time we learned anything about what was supposedly going on at Deepcut was when we turned on the news in the evening to see him telling the media.

A week later, when Frank had finished 'investigating' James's death, he eventually did phone me. I was in the car with Jim, Claire and Stuart, and we were driving from a restaurant, as Stuart had wanted to treat us to a nice celebratory meal in Dundee, having recently got himself his first-ever job. We'd had a lovely evening when the mobile phone rang. Frank said that from the tests he had conducted, James's wounds 'may well have been self-inflicted, but as a result of an accident'. I couldn't take it in and was quite confused. For all his talk and all his promises, Frank was now concluding the opposite to his initial theory. He then bamboozled us with science about the experiments, as if trying to back up his conclusions, but to be honest I was so shocked I don't think I was listening. When we ended the call, we were all terribly upset and it had ruined our evening out.

Back at the house, Jim called Frank to hear the news for himself. Frank said he had spoken to one of the senior officers at Deepcut that day and asked him how he would feel if he concluded James's death was just an accident. The officer, he claimed, then said, 'Perfect, that's exactly what we want to hear.' This second phone call with Frank was even more confusing than the first, and we couldn't grasp what it was he was trying to tell us. It was as if he were trying to play mind games with us.

However, the next time we saw Frank in person, he had changed his mind. 'Remember when I said James's wounds were self-inflicted?' he said. 'Well, don't believe it. Your son's wounds weren't self-inflicted. I only told you that over the phone to prove whether or not your phones were being bugged. And what I told you ended up in the newspapers, so someone must have been listening. That's the only reason I told you all that. The reality is they were not self-inflicted. Some other person was there.'

I don't think I could have been any angrier with Frank.

I couldn't understand why someone we had put so much faith and trust in would do this to us. Why would he say our son's death was self-inflicted and let us believe that for weeks? As we sat there, I honestly thought he was sick in the head. You just don't say things like that to a bereaved parent. Not to us, anyway. It was cruel. We didn't know what to believe, and inside I was aching. Part of me wanted to end the relationship there and then and walk away, but another part of me wondered if perhaps Frank was simply telling us the truth that we didn't want to hear. After a great deal of soul-searching, we decided to give him the benefit of the doubt, for the time being anyway.

On 27 February 2003, Frank Swann left Deepcut the same way he went in: with a posse of journalists hanging on his every word. Outside the gates, with Geoff Gray standing by his side, he dramatically announced that he knew how our loved ones died but would only reveal all at a later date. Asked whether the wounds were caused by another person or as the result of an accident, he replied to one reporter, 'We do know the answer, but we cannot say.' He went on to say he had used a metal detector to search for missing bullets in the ground, fired more than 800 rounds from an SA-80 gun, and used animal blood on the rifles to determine whether the firearms had been moved after death.

The press lapped it up and the coverage the next day was screaming for a public inquiry. Frank Swann had cracked it, or so the public thought. We knew different, however, and behind the scenes I was still questioning whether Frank genuinely knew what he was talking about. Yes, I'd given him the benefit of the doubt, but at the back of my mind, I had to take everything he said with a pinch of salt. We had seen coverage on the television news of him carrying out his supposed scientific tests, some of which appeared to be done on the type of polystyrene trays used for takeaway food. It looked too unprofessional for me to truly believe he had found all the answers that Surrey Police hadn't.

It took Frank another five months to release his findings to the public. He announced that Sean Benton, Cheryl James and Geoff Gray could not have killed themselves, and even claimed Cheryl had been pushing the gun away from her face at the time of her death. In our case, however, he said James's death was 'inconclusive'. It was a cop-out.

We had prepared ourselves for this conclusion, given Frank's conflicting findings and confusion earlier in the year. One minute it was murder, the next it was accidental, then he said there was someone else at the scene, and now he just didn't know. You would have thought we'd have been devastated, but it simply summed up our dealings with Frank Swann. We were disappointed, of course we were, but more so at the fact he had wasted almost a year of our lives. For nothing.

Part of me wonders if Frank failed to come up with a conclusion because James had undergone two post-mortems and, in theory anyway, his body was still available for further testing if required. In contrast, the bodies of Geoff Gray and Sean Benton had been cremated, while the parents of Cheryl James said they would never consider exhuming their daughter. In other words, Frank Swann's findings could have been scientifically proved wrong as far as our son's death was concerned, but not in the other three cases. Indeed, in the years that followed so many other experts have cast doubt on his conclusions. Frank did tell us that, in his opinion, although the wound was consistent with self-infliction, the gunpowder tattooing on James's chin was not, and neither was the pattern of the blood on the ground. He also claimed that if James had committed suicide, there should have been another patch of blood on the ground beside his body, and the fact that there wasn't suggested that another person had been kneeling down in front of him pulling the trigger. It was mere speculation and didn't do much for us. He might as well have said Colonel Mustard did it with the candlestick in the library.

For the other families, however, Frank's conclusions spurred them on, and they were even more convinced that their loved ones hadn't killed themselves. They were over the moon, in fact, and it really helped the campaign for a public inquiry. I knew I had to hide my own disappointment and keep my reservations about Frank to myself, because, no matter what I thought, at that particular time he was helping the cause.

Looking back on it today, though, I honestly feel Frank was talking nonsense. Put it this way: he only submitted one single piece of paper as 'evidence' to Surrey Police – nothing more. He did it on the eve of the publication of the force's own report into Deepcut, thus prompting officials to delay their findings by months, much to the frustration of the families. If his announcement was deliberately timed to annoy the police as much as possible, he had succeeded.

Frank released no more information. There was nothing about what he had done inside Deepcut, no detail about how he had come to his conclusions, and no evidence of any sort to back up his theories. Instead, he said that a set of compact discs containing his full findings and the breakdown of all his tests had been posted to the four corners of the world, and would only ever be published upon his death. You've got to ask yourself why.

Frank later sent each of the families a special file about his month-long visit to Deepcut, but I can only describe it as laughable. Inside there was only one single sheet of A4 pertaining to James, and even then, halfway through it Frank started referring to our son as Geoff and muddled up all manner of things. He mentioned that James died from one bullet wound to the head – which was correct – and then went on about two wounds a few sentences later. The document wasn't even spell-checked. It was a cut-and-paste job of the worst kind and a total embarrassment to him and to us, and I think we cried when we read through it. The file contained images of Frank posing with a gun and photographs of his caravan laboratory. If all this wasn't bad enough, he had arranged for it to be sent to us by Special Delivery on 24 December 2003. Merry Christmas, indeed.

That was the final straw for us. Frank Swann had played mind games with us once too often. We had enough to contend with in life without someone else messing about with us and leading us on a merry dance. It was clear to us that our involvement with this man had been a complete waste of time, and the Grays now felt the same.

We didn't hear from Frank again after that Christmas Eve, but we chose not to chastise him in the media for the rubbish he had sent to us. We were better than that. Our solicitor agreed with us, and we simply took the decision to end all contact with him.

In hindsight, I feel the Deepcut families were taken advantage of. We were people in need, and along came a man who saw an opportunity and took it. Frank Swann gained a lot of publicity over the years – as well as some healthy fees for appearing on television so frequently – but as far as I am concerned that's all he got, because he never came up with any answers. Indeed, I've seen him quoted in various newspapers since then bleating on about how he has lost work and been dropped from police and local authority jobs as a result of his association with the Deepcut families. It's little wonder, if you ask me. I'm certain the police and the Army were laughing at us all behind our backs for having employed Frank in the first place.

Eleven years on, if I could turn the clock back to that first meeting with Frank Swann, I would walk away. It all sounded too good to be true, and it was. I have never seen any evidence from him to back up his theories, and I am not convinced the CDs he claims he has contain any proof, or even exist, for that matter.

What I do know, however, is that Frank Swann broke our hearts. He made a mockery of himself and our campaign, and what he gained from it all I will never know. It was a macabre charade. Oh how we regret ever laying eyes on that man.

13. Towers of Strength

The Deepcut Four. It had a certain ring to it, and I have to confess I liked that description of us the first time I saw it used in a newspaper. No longer was it just Yvonne and Jim against the world; we also had Des and Doreen James, Geoff and Diane Gray, and Harry and Linda Benton. Four bereaved families. Four dead soldiers. Four reasons for a public inquiry to take place.

There were lots of tears that first time we all met up at Kevin McNamara's Westminster office back in June 2002. We shared stories and swapped photographs of our loved ones, and it was a nice feeling to have companionship and strength in numbers. There was also an instant bond between us, and we didn't feel like strangers. I felt as if I was being reunited with long-lost friends, as if I'd known each of the others for years. The truth is there is only one person who can truly understand how a bereaved parent is feeling, and that is another bereaved parent. For the eight of us, that sense of understanding ran even deeper, because we had all lost a child in almost the same set of circumstances and at the same Army barracks. What's more, we'd also had similar experiences at the hands of the police and the Ministry of Defence. In many ways, we fuelled each other's fires.

Facing the media that day was a terrifying experience, and we were all extremely nervous. We knew we had to give the impression that we were confident and assured, but the fact is we were scared and unsure what to do. While we could easily talk about our loss and our loved ones, we didn't really know very much about the political process or how we would go about ensuring that justice was done. It was quite daunting standing in a room packed with journalists and MPs, and it reminded me of a scene from a Hollywood movie, or one of those press conferences you often see on TV as some actor or other promotes his latest blockbuster. Flashbulbs from cameras were going off all over the place and reporters jostled for position as we entered the room. Up until that point, I was only used to being interviewed by journalists one to one in the house, so to say the press conference was intimidating is an understatement, to say the least. When it was over, we felt a great sense of relief and had to head to the nearest bar for a drink.

For the parents of Cheryl James and Sean Benton, who had rarely given any interviews, the whole process was even more surreal and very difficult to deal with. Both Jim and I and the Grays had limited experience in dealing with the media, but this was all new to the Jameses and the Bentons. Afterwards, Des James actually gave me praise for the way he thought I was handling the pressure so soon after losing my son. If only he'd known how I felt inside.

Harry and Linda Benton hadn't really spoken about their personal tragedy in public before, even though seven years had now passed. Reliving the day they lost their son for the assembled media was clearly painful for them.

Private Sean Harry Benton's death on 9 June 1995 was the first of the four shootings at the barracks. Slightly older than the others, at twenty, he was found with five bullet wounds to his chest. Unusually, the shots came in two separate bursts of automatic fire, one on each side of his body. Three of the bullets were fired at close range into his left side and two from further away into his right side. Witnesses said Sean had gone to the guardroom and convinced another soldier to give him her gun by telling her a sergeant wanted to see her. A few moments later, gunfire was heard from near the Officers' Mess and Sean was dead.

Despite the multiple shots, the initial assumption by the Army was suicide. Certainly, there was evidence to suggest Sean had been bullied quite severely during his short time in the Army – he had signed up in June 1994 when he was 19 – and he had already made several attempts to take his life at Deepcut. However, what sowed the seeds of doubt with his family was the fact he'd had his passport on him when he died, suggesting he was set to go AWOL from the camp: that he was going to run away from his tormentors rather than end his life. Also in his possession was a letter addressed to his parents in East Sussex saying that he couldn't stand Army life any more and telling them how sorry he was that he had let them down. Defence officials assumed it was a suicide note, but there is nothing contained in it that proves conclusively that Sean was about to kill himself.

It was only five months later that 18-year-old Welsh girl Cheryl James, another private, was found dead not far from the spot that Sean had died. On the morning of 27 November 1995, she had been on lone patrol with a loaded weapon – something that is against Army regulations – and was discovered with a single gunshot wound to the head. Her body was found in woodland just a few yards outside the perimeter fence, not far from the entrance to the barracks. She had only been at Deepcut for 11 days.

During the post-mortem that followed, the bullet was removed from her brain but then lost, meaning there is no proof that it was even from the gun she was carrying.

As was the case with the other deaths, no forensic tests were carried out, no fingerprints were taken, and no police investigation was initiated. It was another case of 'one bullet, one body, draw your own conclusion'.

Adding to the general theory of suicide, the Army's review of Cheryl's death – written up by the base commander just three weeks after the tragedy, and a week before the coroner had even opened the official inquest into the shooting – told how she had found the barracks tough. She had been suffering problems in her love life and was told off for chatting to her boyfriend – a fellow private at Deepcut – as she carried out her guard duties shortly before she died. She had also recently been put on two minor charges for entering a restricted area and subsequently failing to attend a punishment parade. As far as the Army was concerned, Cheryl James was a classic troubled soul.

However, her parents, from Llangollen in north Wales, were not convinced and tried every avenue they could to show there was more to their daughter's death. Des spent years as a lone voice against the Establishment without success, and the stress eventually took its toll on him. There came a point at which he and Doreen decided they'd simply had enough of hitting brick walls and gave up; they lost hope of ever finding out the truth behind Cheryl's shooting. In many ways, I think they were buoyed the most by the fact that there were now three other families in the same position as them. Indeed, when Surrey Police later announced it was going to reinvestigate her death and that of Sean Benton after all those years, they were elated. Finally they would get answers. Finally they would hear how, and why, their daughter died.

By the time we stood together as the Deepcut Four for the first time, I was already very familiar with Geoff and Diane Gray. Fewer than three months had passed since

Geoff had left that note for me at the mortuary, but we'd managed to build up a good relationship. As a result of this, I think the other two families looked towards us for guidance and support as far as the media was concerned, at least in the early days. Certainly, the deaths of our children were the most recent and, arguably, had the most in common.

Like my James, Private Geoff Gray was only 17 when he was found dead at Deepcut on the night of 17 September 2001. The Army said he had shot himself in the head with his SA-80 rifle twice. In another similarity to our case, he had also been on guard duty and had been patrolling the same small perimeter fence that surrounded the Officers' Mess as James had when he died. What was strange about Geoff's death, though, was that his body wasn't found during an initial sweep of the area, only to be discovered at a spot that soldiers insisted they had already searched three times.

Like us, the Grays did not believe the official version of events put forward by the Army and insisted their son would not have killed himself: he had everything to live for. In the days that followed the tragedy, desperate for information, Diane had called Deepcut and asked if there was any update on the investigation into their son's death, just as Jim did six months later. She was told something along the lines of, 'For goodness' sake, Mrs Gray, your son killed himself. Now get over it.'

Geoff and Diane were given no further details on what happened and there was no Army investigation, never mind any involvement from police. It was only six months later, on the day of the coroner's inquest – a hearing that lasted just three hours – that they learned for the first time that their son had actually been shot twice. He had two bullet wounds to the head, and no one had bothered to tell them.

The Grays wrote letters to every single Member of Parliament demanding an investigation, but their heartfelt plea fell upon deaf ears. No one was prepared to listen. As far as the politicians were concerned, it looked like the Grays' son had shot himself and, as tragic as it was, that was that. Geoff and Diane were at their wits' end, so when they learned of another shooting at Deepcut and heard the name James Collinson for the first time, it gave them fresh hope of uncovering some answers about their own son's untimely death.

I'll never forget the first meeting Jim and I had with the Grays at their home in Hackney, London. It had been arranged by the BBC in May 2002 for the first *Frontline Scotland* programme about the Deepcut deaths, and it's fair to say it was an emotional affair. The Grays had a great deal of empathy for what we were going through, and while they had suffered a loss of their own, I found them more supportive of us than anything else. From the very outset, they showed themselves as very caring and compassionate people. They still are.

We were both at different stages of the grieving process: Jim and I were still feeling the rawness of James's loss and anger towards the Army, but the Grays had moved on a little from that and were ready to start their search for answers. We complemented one another. While only about seven months had passed since their son's death, Geoff and Diane had been through a hell of a lot in that short space of time. For instance, during the coroner's inquest into the shooting, which was held just a few days before our James died, Geoff was not even given permission to have a lawyer present and had to represent himself. A caretaker by trade, he was forced to stand there in court and question witnesses, including Army top brass. Worse still, he was only given the case notes an hour before the hearing started.

When we met the Grays for the first time, we devised an early strategy about what we should be doing to raise awareness of the two deaths, such as finding a solicitor to represent us and getting the media on our side. Thereafter, as we put the plan into action, we had daily phone calls and email updates, and we supported one another during TV and newspaper interviews at every opportunity. At that point, the campaign was still low-key, because we weren't aware of the other two families yet, but had it not been for the Grays and the effort they put in at the beginning, I don't think there would have been a campaign at all.

While I do think the Bentons and the Jameses probably benefited the most in the early days from being the Deepcut Four, there is no denying that both Geoff and Diane and Jim and I got a major boost from it too. We had all experienced the difficulty and isolation of searching for the truth as individuals, and we knew that together, as a group of four, we had a more powerful case. One unexplained death at an Army barracks barely raised an eyebrow, but four – well, that was a scandal. In that sense, none of the families tried to push their own personal crusade ahead of the group as a whole. We understood that we all needed one another.

The four families were in contact fairly regularly after that first joint meeting in London, but the overall thrust and strategy of the campaign was devised between Geoff and me during our daily phone calls and emails.

We didn't have defined roles set out within the group, except that we would each deal with any issues arising within our geographical areas. For Jim and I, that obviously meant ensuring we kept in touch with politicians in Scotland and being available for any Scottish media interviews.

However, it wasn't long before we crowned Geoff our

unofficial group leader. It wasn't anything to do with his case being any more important than the others; rather it was because his location, in the heart of London, made him more accessible to the media. He had the BBC, ITN and Sky News on his doorstep, and it made sense for him to be rolled out at short notice for a comment on Deepcut whenever one was needed. We also felt Geoff came across better during interviews than the rest of us, and he seemed to enjoy it, considering the circumstances. Indeed, during the first few months of the campaign for a public inquiry, I think he spent more time in television studios than he did at work.

If Geoff was revelling in his media appearances and his frequent verbal attacks on the Army, in stark contrast the Bentons hated every moment of being in the limelight. We didn't often see them, and while they backed the calls for a public inquiry, they shied away from being at the forefront of the campaign. People cope with grief differently and they chose to stay very private, and we all respected that. To my knowledge, the Bentons never tried to argue Sean didn't commit suicide. Any time I spoke to Linda and Harry, they always said they feel more that the Army failed their son. He was clearly having problems during his spell at Deepcut – he was treated for a number of self-harm incidents and underwent psychiatric treatment – but the question is how much of this was as a result of being bullied? Sean Benton went in to the Princess Royal Barracks a happy-go-lucky lad and came out in a coffin. Why?

As the months passed, the four families worked well together as a group, and we became more like friends than fellow campaigners. Apart from the obvious, we had a lot in common and we enjoyed a great rapport. Of course, it was hard work fighting against officialdom on a daily basis, but we had some laughs and good times along the way: it wasn't all sadness and tears. Meetings between us usually took place in offices at Westminster, where it had all started, and in the first year alone Jim and I went up and down to London from Perth more than 30 times. The pair of us would stay at Geoff and Diane's house in Hackney when we travelled south, and we came to know it as our home from home. We were put up in a bunk bed in Geoff junior's room, and on one occasion the Grays even put a sign on the door that read 'The Collinson Suite'. They always made us feel so welcome, with Diane regularly cooking us a hearty meal and Geoff ferrying us around in his car.

Geoff liked to record the group press conferences and any television interviews we did in London for us all to analyse afterwards. It was a kind of homework exercise used to help make us all better at talking to the media. I remember on one occasion Geoff being furious following a press call at Westminster because he'd spotted Harry Benton chewing gum as the camera panned across to him. 'You can't be chewing gum! That's so unprofessional,' he ranted at the television as we watched the footage back. However, as the camera went further along the room, it stopped on Geoff himself, who had a cigarette tucked behind an ear. I laughed so hard as we watched him squirm in his seat. Our relationship with the Grays was often like that: one minute there would be tears and sadness as we recalled our loved ones, but then the next we'd be in hysterics at something funny.

I'm not sure when the transition happened but we became best friends. Certainly, I saw more of Geoff and Diane than I did of my real family, and away from the television cameras and the next round of newspaper interviews we had fun and we enjoyed their company. We exchanged birthday and Christmas presents, knew all of their extended family, and even became sociable with their neighbours. It was just a shame that it had taken the deaths of our sons to bring us together in the first place.

The families rarely disagreed, but Geoff and I developed differing views in 2003 about the creation of a bigger campaigning group called Deepcut and Beyond. Its aim was to force a public inquiry not only into our four deaths but also into all unexplained combat and non-combat deaths within the Armed Forces. In my opinion, the group became too big too quickly – more than 50 different families joined up to lobby the government at one point – and it moved the focus away from James, Geoff, Cheryl and Sean. I did have sympathy for all these other bereaved parents, and I was certain many of the cases warranted proper investigation. But I believed that if we were to ask the Ministry of Defence for an inquiry into every single slightly suspicious death in the last 20 years, we would get turned down instantly. It would be unrealistic to expect anything less. When there was just the four families putting the pressure on for a public inquiry into the deaths of our four children, there was always a possibility we might win. When everyone else with a connection to a sudden death got on board, we were doomed. Geoff couldn't see that, though, and we agreed to disagree on the issue. We still do.

The constant campaigning was tough. It was very draining, both emotionally and physically, for each of the families to think of nothing but Deepcut and how we could force a public inquiry. Most of us suffered from ill health and periods of depression when we just thought, 'I can't go on.' However, when times got tough, we became towers of strength for one another. When another door was slammed in our faces, we needed the love and support of the others to keep us strong and positive. As the years passed, there were so many opportunities for us to walk away, to give up and move on with our lives, but no one ever took them. With each disappointment, with each knock-back, we simply rallied round and got on with the job at hand. After all, if we gave up on our loved ones, who else was going to carry the mantle? That's what got us through the rocky periods.

Mind you, at times it was extremely difficult. Each of the families went through the most unimaginable torment and endured things that no one should ever have to suffer. Geoff and Diane, for instance, had to endure the horror of being told that part of their son's skull had lain in a field for months before being found. Des and Doreen were already living with the agony of knowing Cheryl might have been a target for sexual harassment when they were informed by Frank Swann that he believed their beloved daughter had tried to push the gun away in her last moments. The Bentons were learning, almost by the day, new details about the extent to which their son had been suffering at the hands of violent bullies. For Jim and me, I don't think we will ever overcome the fact we exhumed our son's body.

As a parent, all you ever want to do is protect your child, yet none of us were there to prevent the deaths of our children. We all felt that pain so deeply. Indeed, we felt it for one another. Whenever anything traumatic happened to one of the families, we all felt the blow; we all shared the hurt. We had that kind of close bond.

My relationship with Jim often confused people, because it must have looked, at least publicly, like we were still a married couple. In the early days of the campaign, we spent almost every hour of every day together despite our separation, and during every interview and at every photo opportunity we would be seen side by side. Yet we weren't together: I had Malcolm. This led to odd moments of awkwardness, of course, for example when photographers would ask me and Jim to cuddle or hold hands. We played along for the cameras, though: we might not have been husband and wife, but we were still James's mum and dad. It amuses me now to think that because of this, some sections of the media thought we were very much a couple during the height of the campaign. I am reliably informed that the penny only dropped for some national newspapers when it emerged I was getting married to someone else!

We hadn't always been so convivial, however. When our marriage collapsed in 2000, Jim and I were, at times, like any other couple who had fallen out of love, and as the weeks and months passed after our separation, a great deal of animosity developed between us. I had instigated divorce proceedings a few days before James died, and Jim was still coming to terms with that as he then tried to cope with the loss of his son. It was only in the immediate aftermath of James's death that our attitude changed: the tension between us evaporated as we focused all our energies on dealing with our personal tragedy. I even postponed the divorce proceedings. If Malcolm was my rock during the heartache of March 2002, then I have to say that I was Jim's, and had it not been for me, I'm not sure how he would have coped. I'm glad to say we have had a good relationship since that terrible day we learned our son was dead.

The experiences shared by the four families as we strived for a public inquiry throughout 2002 became the basis for two critically acclaimed theatre productions six years later. *Geoff Dead: Disco for Sale*, written by Fiona Evans, was centred on Geoff and Diane's story and the trauma they went through in the aftermath of learning their son had died. It made mention of the other sets of parents, including us, and focused particularly on the way in which we had all been treated with utter disdain by the Army. The unusual title of the play was inspired by Geoff senior's visit to the local newspaper office to ask about putting a death notice in the obituaries column. At the reception, he was told the first five words of the tribute were free and, partly being sarcastic and partly attempting to hide his pain, he had replied, 'Fabulous. How about "Geoff Dead: Disco for Sale"?' Despite the name, it was a very moving and powerful play and really did the Grays justice.

The other play was called *Deep Cut* and was written by Philip Ralph, who ended up winning a number of awards for the production. It was very different to *Geoff Dead: Disco for Sale* and was based around the personal experience of Des and Doreen James. The story centred on the long fight for justice they had endured since 1995, from the moment their daughter died right up to the first days of the campaign for a public inquiry. It was heart-rending stuff and it opened to five-star reviews, with one in *The Observer* even saying it was 'theatre at its most powerful, political and important'.

I saw the play numerous times, and each night I watched people leave the theatre in tears, bewildered at the scale of the injustice against the Deepcut families. They didn't know the half of it.

14. On the Brink of Victory

I wasn't sure what I was supposed to do to mark the first anniversary of James's death, on 23 March 2003. I had been dreading that day coming for months, more or less since the turn of the New Year, and I was worried that I wouldn't be able to cope, particularly because every movement we made was now carried out in the glare of the media spotlight. Should we go to church? Should we host a quiet gathering? Should we go to the graveside? Should we leave town and avoid everyone? I honestly didn't know.

The looming anniversary wasn't made any easier when, days beforehand, we unexpectedly took delivery of James's possessions from Deepcut. We were given no warning, and it came as a surprise to find an Army official at Jim's front door holding two brown cardboard boxes. It was the same visiting officer who had delivered the news of James's death to Jim a year earlier, and now here he was back again delivering his belongings. The man came in, dumped the boxes on the hall floor and said, 'There you go,' before shaking our hands, turning around and walking straight back out of the door. The whole process lasted about 20 seconds.

We opened the first box, which contained nothing but coat hangers of all shapes and sizes. Inside the second box were clothes, shoes, a mini CD player, James's watch, and other bits and pieces, not neatly packed but rather all thrown in without any care or attention. It was as if someone had slid their arm along a row of James's belongings and swept them into an empty box. There was no sign of his wallet or his passport, and there were no personal letters or photographs, or any of his toiletries. What's more, the items inside the box were dirty. One blue towel I had washed and dried on the day James died was filthy and had a muddy boot print in the middle, as if it had been stood on and used to clean the floor. I felt as if someone had given us a hard slap across the face, and it showed a complete lack of respect to us and to James's memory.

We vented our anger at Surrey Police, and after the family liaison officers went off to ask questions at Deepcut, we learned that many of James's other possessions had been destroyed, including his letters. The Army said they didn't want to cause us any offence by seeing anything belonging to James that, in their opinion, he wouldn't have wanted his family to see. For example, they said he had condoms in his wallet, so they took it upon themselves not to remove them, but instead to destroy the wallet 'as a matter of procedure'. His passport was posted back to the passport office, and not to us, his next of kin, while his bank cards were dispatched to his bank to be cut up. His new driving licence had also arrived at the barracks after his death, but that, too, was never seen again. The Army had systematically erased every last moment of James's existence. How dare they? What right did they have? He was our son, not theirs, and it only added insult to injury.

We didn't really need the first anniversary of James's death to remind us of what we had lost. The pain of not having him with us was, and still is, something that lives with us all on a daily basis. If I'm honest, I still don't think I have fully accepted the fact I will never see him again.

Even now, any time I see a group of teenagers I look for him, half expecting to see James there, only to realise all over again that he's not. At times, I also have this strange feeling of hope that he is about to come walking through the door again. But he's not. He's dead. That heartache never goes away. It's unbearable.

When the anniversary itself came, I had psyched myself up for it so much that it wasn't as bad as I had imagined it would be. The sun still rose in the morning, the birds still sang, and life carried on as normal. It was an ordinary day like every other. Our postman was heavily laden with cards and letters of support from those who had remembered the significance of the date, and it was lovely that people were thinking of us. I was actually working at Almondbank House on 23 March 2003, and while I did turn up for my shift, my mind wasn't on the job. James was uppermost in my thoughts throughout the day. I still had so many questions a full year on from the shooting, but I didn't have the answer to any of them.

In the end, we chose to go to the cemetery in the evening and have some quiet time to ponder the 12 months that had passed, and that was about it. It wasn't a day to celebrate; it was a day for reflection, and that's what we did.

We had been kept busy in the three months leading up to the anniversary, what with our day-to-day campaigning and Frank Swann's dramatic announcement to the media that he knew how our loved ones had died. However, there were other, far more sinister, developments.

Towards the end of January, we had the house in Perth swept for surveillance devices amid mounting suspicion we were being bugged. Information that only a handful of people within the campaign group knew had been turning up in newspapers over the months, such as the fact we were going to exhume James's body. We had told no one about that, yet it was all over the media. Frank Swann had also planted seeds of doubt about the security of our telephone when he had suggested the lines were tapped, and on occasions we would hear odd noises. I remember during one phone call to Diane Gray, we both clearly heard a female voice on the line whispering, 'Did you get that?'

It does sound utterly ridiculous: I mean, who would want to bug us? But we got in touch with the family liaison officers, and they arranged for Tayside Police to come to the house and carry out tests. It came as a great shock when the officers said they had picked up signals from what they described as 'receivers' in the lamp and in the phone. They offered to take them away, but, strange as it may sound, I insisted we keep the devices: if I was being bugged, I wanted the people doing it to be aware we knew about it. We were then given advice about turning the kitchen tap on full to add background noise if we wanted to talk about anything personal. Down in London, similar tests were carried out at Geoff and Diane's house, and while the police found nothing, the Grays were issued with panic alarms connecting them straight to the Metropolitan Police for their own security.

Jim and I took the decision to let the *Sunday Express* know about the visit from Tayside Police and what they had found. They were most interested, and days later, the word 'BUGGED' screamed out from the newspaper's front page in the biggest headline I had ever seen. If the people listening into us hadn't known we'd found out, well, they did now.

The story caused quite a stir, and within days MPs had raised questions in the House of Commons about the alleged surveillance operation. The government denied it had anything to do with the Ministry of Defence or with the Security Services, but you have to ask yourself, who else has the capability to put devices in a phone and a lamp in our living room without our being aware of it? Even today, I still can't understand why anyone would want to listen in to us. Whoever it was, I just wish they would acknowledge it and say sorry.

Strange things were also happening with our emails, and we had that investigated by Surrey Police. For example, we regularly had emails go automatically into the junk basket, which is a common occurrence with spam filters, except that in our case the messages had also already been opened. In addition, other people would receive nasty emails from my account that were categorically not sent by me. A woman called Jan Manship-Milligan, who lost her son Alfie in mysterious circumstances and was one of the Deepcut and Beyond mothers, said I had sent her a message accusing her of jumping on the bandwagon and telling her to drop her campaign. I did not send it, yet there it was with my name and my correct email address on it. The same kinds of things were happening with Geoff and Diane Gray's email account. It made no sense whatsoever.

Life had become fairly surreal for me and Jim by the time the first anniversary arrived. A year earlier we had been going about our dull, day-to-day lives and James was preparing himself for the next stage of his Army training. Now James was dead, we were in newspapers and on television across the world every other day, we were fronting a campaign that saw us at Westminster more times than some MPs, and, it would seem, we were being bugged in the process. If you could have wound back the clock to 22 March 2002 and told me all this was about to happen to me, I would not have believed you.

We were in constant demand in the days after the anniversary. The phone never stopped ringing, and journalists were at the front door in their droves as we did interview after interview. It got to the stage where Stuart and Claire got used to coming home from school only to find the house had been taken over by another camera crew. It was never-ending, and at one point I had to go to the doctor to help me overcome the exhaustion of being constantly on the go and surviving on two hours' sleep a night.

Jim and I still enjoyed a great relationship with the media a year down the line, and we were happy to oblige with every request. As big a story as Deepcut was, we knew that interest in James and in the deaths in general wouldn't last forever, and we had to capitalise on every opportunity provided to us to keep them at the forefront of people's minds. As the months had passed we had become more experienced at dealing with reporters, and we learned how to be more comfortable in front of the camera. I have looked back at some of our first appearances on television and they are cringe-worthy, with Jim unshaven and the pair of us looking a bit unkempt. By March 2003, we were more professional-looking and were speaking more clearly and confidently, with Jim usually sporting a suit and tie. In a strange way, we'd become used to being media figures and being at the beck and call of journalists, and we accepted that people might point at us in the street because they recognised us. That was fine: anything that raised the profile of the campaign had to be welcomed.

The first-ever live interview I did was with John Stapleton and Penny Smith on *GMTV* in the London studios, not long after James died. It was a daunting prospect, because I normally watched that show in the morning and I was familiar with the presenters, yet here I was about to sit on that famous sofa and be interviewed by them. Worse still, I was on my own for the first time and didn't have Jim or one of the other families beside me for back-up. A chauffeur-driven car collected me from Geoff Gray's house, and backstage I shared the Green Room with the famous boy band Westlife. It was a whole new world to me. I was a nervous wreck, and I think it showed. The experience wasn't helped when, moments before we went on air, the *GMTV* lawyers warned me about making wild accusations or saying anything that might get them in trouble on live television. It made me over-cautious, and in the end I said very little at all.

When I went back to Geoff's house afterwards for his usual video debrief, I was horrified and decided there and then that I had to make an effort to become more confident on TV. I'm glad I did, because there were many more television and radio appearances to come, including on Sky News, BBC1, BBC2, ITV, Channel 5, Radio 1 and Five Live. Then there were the documentaries, including the two *Frontline Scotland* programmes, *Tonight with Trevor McDonald* and *Panorama*. As far as the print media was concerned, in the first year of the campaign we appeared in every single British newspaper, and I even learned of snippets appearing in the press and on websites in New York, Australia and India.

One of my fondest memories – if you can use that word to describe how it felt to be on live TV talking about the death of your son – came during an appearance on *Richard & Judy* on Channel 4 in October 2002. Jim and I were treated like celebrities, with our own wardrobe assistant and make-up person and even a dressing room with our names on the door. We didn't revel in it, because we knew well that we were only there because our son had died, but it was nice to be treated with such respect all the same. Before the show went live, Richard Madeley came to see us and say hello. As he walked in through the dressing room door, I got up to shake his hand and introduce myself. He replied, 'Yes, I know who you are: I've seen you on television.' I laughed and still find that little exchange amusing.

On the show that night were David Baddiel and Vanessa Feltz, who was a lovely lady and took a genuine interest in our campaign. It was the day after we had exhumed James's body, and when Jim and I were being interviewed, the entire production crew stood at the sides watching and listening before disappearing when the other two guests came on. After the show, Richard and Judy presented us with a small gift and wrote a short note saying they supported our cause and telling us to keep up the good work. It was a real boost.

There is a common misconception that we were paid to go on all these television and radio shows, or were given fees for the interviews in the press. Even some of our own family and friends presumed we were making vast sums of money, but we weren't. Our only reward for being on TV or in a newspaper was the coverage and getting our story across to more people. The truth is, our media appearances and the constant campaigning actually cost us money and led to bankruptcy. Very few people know this, because we chose to keep our private affairs private. Because we hadn't been back at work in months, any money we did have prior to James's death dwindled away on travelling expenses, new clothes for being on television or general day-to-day living. We then racked up huge debts on mail-order catalogues because we had no other way of paying for clothes, and credit cards were used to cover our travelling expenses. By July 2003 we had no money left, and the family home on Colonsay Street, the house where James grew up, was repossessed. It was heartbreaking. I already had a council flat of my own, with Malcolm and the boys – Stuart had also moved in by then – but Jim had nowhere to go. Claire came to live with me while Jim went to live in a bed and breakfast as he waited to be allocated a flat by the council. All the furniture went into storage. It was a difficult time for us, but we pulled together and got through it.

We didn't have that much time to stop and mull over the loss of the family home in any case, because the campaign juggernaut was gathering pace. More MPs had backed our demands for a public inquiry, greater numbers of people were coming forward to lobby the government, and charities and campaigning groups such as Amnesty International came out in support of us. Some 4,000 readers of the *Sunday Express* had also now backed the newspaper's Justice for James crusade, and the coupons had been posted off to Downing Street. It felt like the entire country was behind us, pushing us forward. The only ones against a public inquiry were the Army and Tony Blair's Labour government.

On 8 May 2003, Jim and I joined Geoff and Diane in a silent protest outside Deepcut on the day of a visit by Princess Anne, the patron of the Royal Logistic Corps. Dressed in black funeral attire, we stood there with our heads bowed while holding giant photographs of James, Geoff, Sean and Cheryl. As far as we were concerned, it was disrespectful for Anne to be going to the camp at a time when it was under so much scrutiny and embroiled in so many sinister allegations. How on earth could she be in there sipping cups of tea and telling everyone what a great job they were all doing when the deaths of four soldiers remained unsolved? As the Princess Royal's car drove past, I noticed her looking over at us and I caught her eye. Our point had been made.

It had been a momentous year for us, and as 2003 came to a close, we didn't think there was any way in which Ministers could continue to blank our demands for a public inquiry. We truly believed an announcement was imminent, such was the pressure on the government. We were on the brink of victory.

15. Back to Square One

It was at precisely 10.41 a.m. on 27 April 2004 that the government broke our hearts by officially ruling out a public inquiry into Deepcut for the first time. We had been campaigning for almost two years by this point, but it only took a matter of minutes for the Defence Secretary Geoff Hoon to stand up during a parliamentary debate, address the Commons and say 'no'. It was devastating.

The debate into the growing fiasco surrounding the Princess Royal Barracks was held as a result of pressure from the Liberal Democrat MP Lembit Öpik, and over the course of the 90-minute session, MPs on all sides of the House called for an immediate inquiry.

When Hoon stood up that morning, I was convinced he was about to announce a public inquiry: then, finally, we might get some answers. We all thought the same, as did the media. All the indications were that the government had caved in. Instead, the Defence Secretary brought the whole Deepcut campaign crashing down in 20 minutes flat.

Hoon started by saying he had sympathy for our plight and that he understood our sorrow and our 'desire for answers', as he put it. He said he knew we had been treated with disdain by many quarters. He even said sorry for the shoddy way in which the deaths of James, Geoff, Cheryl and Sean were investigated. But, ultimately, he still said no to a public inquiry.

In his attempt to justify his decision, the Defence Secretary lavished high praise on the British Army, noted that more people under the age of 20 died in the Army as a result of suicide than in civilian life, and insisted that bullying, however abhorrent, was rare. He also bleated on about the increasing ratio of training instructors to recruits now within the UK's barracks. He then concluded, 'What could a narrowly focused inquiry reveal about the circumstances of individual deaths that successive internal and external inquiries have not? What reasonable grounds are there for suspecting that the truth in so far as it is knowable has not already been established?' And that was that. Our two years of hard work and suffering had been for nothing. We were back to square one.

Geoff Hoon's decision was a double blow for us, because it came not long after Surrey Police published its delayed final report into the Deepcut deaths, concluding that all four had been suicides. It came out on 4 March 2004, and each of the families was hand-delivered a copy of the findings shortly before they were made public. I was in London staying with Geoff and Diane, and we had television news crews with us in the living room as we took delivery of the report so that they could get our immediate thoughts on what it contained. The pressure was on us to skim read the twenty-five-page report as fast as possible and then tell the journalists what we thought of almost two years' worth of detective work.

As far as the individual deaths were concerned, the police ruled there was no evidence of any third-party involvement. In other words, our children killed themselves. It was a blow, but, to be honest, we had expected them to come to that conclusion for months. It wasn't a great surprise. I mean, how could they have any evidence? Three of the four deaths hadn't been investigated in the first place, and the probe into James's shooting only started a month after he died, and was calamitous, to say the least.

The report offered a public apology to the families for the police not having taken the lead when it came to looking into the deaths. Surrey Police also apologised for not having ensured 'a thorough investigation from the outset' and acknowledged the fact that they had botched any chance of finding a definitive answer to the four shootings by delaying their inquiries.

The Keystone Cops, as Jim dubbed them, had finally said sorry, and while the public welcomed the apology, it meant nothing to us. It was too little too late. If you think about it, after James died I never had any contact from Surrey Police until I took it upon myself to phone around police stations. Then it emerged evidence had gone missing, some witnesses were never spoken to, the original post-mortem was a sham, and the leads the detectives did get came mainly as a result of suggestions from the families. It was an embarrassment from start to finish.

The main problem was that neither the police nor the Army understood who had the proper jurisdiction to investigate the deaths. Upon each of the bodies being discovered, Surrey Police thought the Army had the lead role and the Army believed the death was being probed by Surrey Police. In the end, with all four deaths, no one actually did anything. I blame the Chief Constable, because that's where the buck stops.

There were positives from the report, however, and I was buoyed by the fact that detectives had uncovered all manner of sinister things going on at Deepcut, and not just relating to the years that our loved ones had been there. What's more, Surrey Police was fairly damning of the Army and the working practices within the Princess Royal Barracks. For instance, the report noted that almost half of all soldiers had witnessed bullying at first hand – with about one in ten having suffered it themselves – and concluded that there was a direct link between Phase 2 training and incidents of self-harm at the camp.

The report also criticised the Army's care regime and said that 'more needed to be done to address areas of risk'. It noted that 'following the involvement of the Deepcut families, the start of the Surrey Police investigation and increasing public scrutiny, a fundamental change occurred in the Army's approach to reducing risks faced by young soldiers and consequently by the Army itself'. However, Surrey Police concluded by calling for a 'broader investigation' that would look at why recruits were particularly vulnerable to undetermined death within Deepcut. It went as far as to say that the government should consider creating an independent body to 'help the Army define and maintain appropriate standards of care for young soldiers'.

While I was disappointed Surrey Police hadn't found out why James died, I was quite excited by their call for an inquiry of sorts and felt positive it would force the government into capitulating to our demands. That's what made Geoff Hoon's decision a month later so hard to swallow.

I simply couldn't get my head around the Defence Secretary's refusal to grant a public inquiry. It was a whitewash as far as I was concerned, and the knock-back had quite an impact on the morale of the families. My life came to a stuttering halt, and I felt as if time was standing still. I took to my bed and remained there for weeks. After two years of fighting, I had flatlined and I didn't know where to go next. I didn't want to speak with anyone and I certainly didn't want to get up, never mind leave the house. I simply curled up in a ball and shut myself off from the world. I was in a dark place and even pondered how I could possibly live without knowing what had happened to James.

In my mind, while I was fighting for justice on James's behalf it made me feel as if I still had a part to play as his mother, that I was able to do something for him even though he was no longer with us. When the Defence Secretary refused a public inquiry, I felt as if he had taken that role away from me. I had become redundant as James's mum; I had let him down and failed him as a mother. In addition, when James died in 2002 I somehow managed to battle through it and suppress much of the grief as I tried to focus all my energies on finding out what had happened to him. With the campaign now seemingly at an end, the reality of it all set in and I couldn't handle the wave of emotion that was pouring over me. In many ways, I started to mourn properly for the first time, and I relived the grief, the anger and the frustration all over again.

Eventually I had to go and see a doctor to get some antidepressants and I was given counselling by the bereavement charity Cruse. That did help, and it enabled me to at least come to terms with what Geoff Hoon had done to us.

It was during this time that my father came back into my life. As I lay in bed with all the dark thoughts floating around my head, I had spent a great deal of time reflecting on my childhood, wondering if all that had happened to me – from the bullies to my uncle's abuse – had somehow resulted in all the negative things I had suffered in recent years. I thought about my dad a lot, and I was curious about whether he was still alive or if he had ever noticed me on the TV or in a newspaper.

I didn't know anything about him, though, apart from a name on a birth certificate. I had only seen him once since the day he walked out on us when I was just over a year old. In 1991, out of the blue, he came up to me in the street in Perth and said, 'Hello. Is your name Yvonne?

I'm your dad.' It was quite a shock, and I stood there with my mouth wide open. After a few brief introductions from Jim to Stuart, James and Claire, who was just a baby at the time, he wandered off and I never heard from him again.

I had never made any previous attempts to contact my dad over the years. I'd always hoped that he would want to find me, then come along and sweep me up in his arms and say 'sorry'. I accept that this was a very romantic notion, but I very much wanted him to want me and show the love a father should show for his daughter. After 30-odd years, when it was clear that this was never going to happen, and that I was living in cloud cuckoo land to expect differently, I should have let go and moved on with my life. But I couldn't. Having lost James, my dad was the one missing piece of the jigsaw of my life and I needed to slot it back in.

I asked my mum and my aunt about the last time they had heard from my dad. Mum was very cautious, because she didn't want me to get hurt any more than I already had been, but in my mind I had been through enough pain in the past two years to know I would be able to cope with being rejected by my father for a second time.

It was Auntie Moira, my mum's sister-in-law, who revealed that the last time she had heard from Dad he was living in England, in a place called Ellesmere Port, near Chester, so I trawled through the phone book and the electoral roll. There were only two William Jeffries. I wrote to both of them, explaining that I was looking for my father and hoped to find out more about my paternal family. Weeks passed without a reply. Yet eventually a letter did arrive from Dad. He told me his life story, saying that he was married and had a son, and that his parents had died, but it was very matter of fact. At the bottom he had signed it 'William Jeffries', not Dad.

As fantastic as it was for him to have been in touch, I was a bit deflated, because I had expected him either to have been pleased to hear from me or to have written back saying he wanted nothing to do with me. Instead, it was somewhere in between, and I didn't know what to do next or whether to write back. Mum did remind me that while he was my father, he was also a stranger, and told me not to expect too much from him, at least in the beginning. I wrote back, and this time around, I received a reply within 48 hours. Better still, it was signed 'Love Dad' and it contained photographs of him and his family. He also said he would like to meet up in Scotland and he included his telephone number.

I waited until there was no one else around in the house before I picked up the phone. I was so nervous, and I didn't want an audience behind me making me any more anxious than I already was. The strange thing is that when he answered, I recognised his voice – or I thought I did anyway. We talked about our lives for what seemed like ages, and he said he had heard about James and was aware of the Deepcut campaign, having seen it on television, but he hadn't realised it was me. He had never known my married name.

Dad said he and his wife were planning a trip to Scotland in September and said that if I wanted to meet face to face, he would be more than delighted. That's what we did, and I met Dad properly for the first time in a restaurant in Perth. It wasn't an emotional reunion as such. Yes, it was nice to finally see him, but it was very formal and we were both still very guarded. We were strangers, after all. At the time, I couldn't feel love towards a man who I didn't know, and, to be honest, I still find it difficult. As I said, I'd had this vision of my father scooping me up in his arms, saying sorry for walking out and telling me everything would be all right because he was now here to protect me and take all my worries away. The reality was that I was faced with an older gentleman in ill health who I didn't know from Adam. He was more in need of looking after than I was.

I discovered I had family I never knew existed, including a half-brother, two stepsisters and two stepbrothers, who all had children of their own. Dad said he had about 28 grandchildren in total at that point, so there were quite a few new names for me to learn.

Meeting my long-lost family was quite exciting, and it gave me a renewed vigour, particularly where Deepcut was concerned. Back in May I had been in bed, refusing to speak to anyone and wondering if I could go on; now I had dozens of new relatives, I was back in contact with my dad and I had much to look forward to. Life was too short to mope around and dwell on the injustice of Geoff Hoon's decision. I had to dust myself down and find a way to fight on.

Within weeks of meeting Dad in Perth, I returned to the campaign in earnest. On 22 October 2004, I went to Kingston-upon-Thames Crown Court in Surrey to watch the sentencing of a 46-year-old former Army officer behind a catalogue of sexual abuse at Deepcut. Leslie Skinner, who was a training instructor, had admitted indecent assaults dating back to 1992 on four young soldiers, aged between 17 and 21. In one of the incidents, a recruit was made to have sex with him, and another victim told how he awoke after a night drinking to find Skinner performing a lewd act on him. The court heard that Skinner, who was married with two children, kept canes and a riding crop in his locker at the barracks, which he used for sexual kicks.

The abuse had only emerged when one of the soldiers, having suffered in silence for years, watched a discussion about male rape on the BBC *Kilroy* programme and contacted the police. It turned out that Surrey Police found it difficult getting the other victims to come forward and had to try to identify them individually from a series of sick photographs found under Skinner's car seat.

I didn't know of Skinner, and his time at the barracks was long before James arrived there, but I wanted to be in court to witness him go to jail, because finally it would allow me to see someone being held to account for his actions. Up until this point, we had only heard anecdotes about abuse at the hands of unnamed officers within the camp.

I went along with Diane Gray and Jim, and the three of us sat in the back row of the public gallery. We didn't want the attention placed on us. Directly in front of us was one of Skinner's victims, who burst into tears as sentencing was passed, and it was sad to see a grown man broken in that way. His ordeal was finally over: for him, justice had been done.

In handing down a four-and-a-half-year-long sentence, the judge was critical of the Army, because it had emerged that officials had known when Skinner was sent to Deepcut that he held a previous conviction for an indecent exposure in Northern Ireland. But instead of being thrown out, when he arrived at the Princess Royal Barracks he was simply demoted to the rank of private. According to the BBC report of the sentencing, Judge Charles Tilling told Skinner, 'For some reason best known to itself the Army then placed you in a position where you were in contact with and had influence over young recruits.'

The court case again highlighted so many failings within Deepcut and the lackadaisical attitude of the Army in general. How could it be that the British Army was fine with letting sex offenders within their midst simply carry on? It wasn't as if they didn't know about convictions: they did, but they chose to turn a blind eye. It was a scandal and raised questions about the calibre of the officers in charge of our soldiers, many of whom are just 17 years old and technically still children. Instructors weren't even checked for criminal records at that time, something that the Deepcut scandal highlighted and has since been remedied by the Army.

While we knew that Skinner was eventually thrown out of the Army in 1998 – he was dismissed after being convicted of indecently assaulting yet another 18-year-old recruit and served six months in jail – we later heard that he rented a cottage on the grounds at Deepcut. For how long I don't know, and we can't be certain whether he was or wasn't there at the time James died. Surrey Police refused to reveal that information to us.

We expected the conviction of Leslie Skinner to be the first of many involving Deepcut officers past and present, and within weeks, more disturbing revelations about the camp emerged. As had been promised back in 2002, the Commons Defence Select Committee had started its own probe into the situation within the Princess Royal Barracks, now that Surrey Police had concluded its investigation. MPs had been passed the full case notes from the police, and they were disturbed to learn that detectives had uncovered more than 100 allegations of serious abuse, bullying, gang rape and other forms of sexual harassment. Worse still, the majority of it had been carried out by NCOs – the officers – on young trainees, both male and female. It was sickening and blew the lid on what had been simmering at Deepcut for years.

The police file – which has still never been made public in its entirety and has not even been seen by the Deepcut families – outlined each of the allegations in detail. For instance, one female recruit claimed she was raped and when she went to report it she was told she would instead be punished for having been in male accommodation. In another incident, a male soldier told detectives about a racist group known as the Black Card Club, whose members would place a card bearing a black cross on the bed of a recruit to be beaten up. Police had also been told how poorly performing trainees were physically assaulted by other recruits sporting respirator masks to hide their identities or forced to parade in the dead of night wearing only their underwear. Others were made to swim in cesspools or forced to stand to attention while officers threw darts at them. There were also more serious allegations that NCOs would abuse their positions of authority to force soldiers into having sex with them in return for giving them an easier life within the barracks.

It was horrific and it turned my stomach. It made me physically sick to think about James being surrounded by all this. The most galling aspect was the fact that clearly the Army top brass could not get a grip on activities that in the civilian world would be criminal offences. Why, we will never know. At least the public finally had evidence of what we had known for years: Deepcut *was* the camp from hell.

16. Corridors of Power

As Jim and I strode across the famous chequered floor of the House of Commons for the umpteenth time in two years, I took a moment to reflect upon just how far we had come since the day we had tentatively ventured inside Britain's political corridors of power for the first time. So much had happened over the course of the past 33 months that I was a different person: that was for sure. The shy grieving mother who had faced the media in the days after James's death was no more, and I was now a confident and knowledgeable campaigner, a woman who felt strangely at ease being in the heart of Westminster.

It was now 1 December 2004, and Jim and I, along with the other Deepcut families, had been summoned before the Commons Defence Select Committee as MPs continued their own investigation into what might be wrong with the Princess Royal Barracks. Two years earlier we would have found the experience daunting – intimidating, even – but we were now so used to dealing with politicians that being at parliament no longer fazed us. Before James died, I don't think I'd ever had any dealings with MPs, and I had them on a pedestal as people to look up to and respect. They were pillars of society, people far higher up the social chain than the likes of Jim and Yvonne Collinson. Now, though, I felt as if I was on a par with them. We were equals.

By this time we had been to Westminster so often we were familiar with the layout of the building and all the parliamentary rules and regulations. Very few people get to see its inner workings, but we knew every nook and cranny – including where all the secret underground passages were located – and we understood what all the bells that rang during the course of the day stood for. We knew the security guards at the entrance and they were getting to know us, and we were on first-name terms with many of the journalists in the media block. To us, the Commons was no longer an iconic place of political power, a building photographed by tourists from around the world. Instead, we viewed it merely as a set of offices and somewhere we had to go when we needed to speak with a politician or bolster our campaign for a public inquiry.

By December 2004, I had actually grown quite comfortable with the constant campaigning and the trips to Westminster in particular. It wasn't because we would be rubbing shoulders with influential people, or because we'd see famous faces in the corridors, but instead because I felt I was doing something for James. He had been gone for almost three years, but by lobbying parliament or addressing the media in London, I was keeping his name alive and I was still being his mum.

Giving evidence to the committee that morning didn't really bolster our campaign and, for the most part, we went over old ground. We spoke about the terrible treatment we'd had from the Army over the years and told the MPs about some of James's possessions being destroyed. Geoff Gray also spoke about how many of his son's belongings were still missing, while Des James said his daughter's diary, which was with her at Deepcut, had vanished and never been located. The Bentons didn't attend the hearing.

As we sat there listening to the MPs debate the issue

amongst themselves, we were able to suss out who was on our side and who wasn't. When we were asked questions by a sympathetic politician, the session was bearable, but when it was someone who disagreed with our demands for a public inquiry, it became tough, and at times we felt as if we were on trial. For instance, I remember Des James standing up on behalf of all the families and asking if the committee was going to bring in the commanding officers at Deepcut – Colonel Ron Laden and Colonel Nigel Josling – and hold them to account. The chairman of the committee, the Labour MP Bruce George, was a formidable and intimidating man, and he angrily chastised poor Des for seemingly insulting his inquiry process. He even insisted he would have 'thrown out' any other group who had questioned his methods as we had done. Mr George added, 'We're taking half our time or more in wondering and agonising what happened to your kids. We're turning down requests to do more inquiries because we feel we have an obligation to your kids and kids who have not been treated well in the Armed Forces.' It was outrageous. I remember thinking that the way he spoke to us, in that condescending tone, it was clear he thought he was doing us a huge favour, out of the goodness of his heart, by looking into Deepcut. Yet he wasn't: it was his job and he was being well paid for it. With some people, we just couldn't win.

Some politicians were helpful; others were particularly obstructive. I have to give the highest praise of all to the Scottish National Party's Annabelle Ewing, who was our local MP in Perth for so many years. She supported us publicly and privately, and was always trying to find new ways to keep James's death on the agenda at Westminster. If we needed political advice she would give it, if we needed a question raised at parliament she would ask it, or if we simply needed a cup of tea and a shoulder to cry on, she would pop around to the house for a chat. We couldn't have asked for more in a Member of Parliament.

Des James's local MP, the Liberal Democrat Lembit Öpik, was also very supportive and made sure his voice was heard whenever it came to Deepcut. He took a great interest in the case – not just for Des and Doreen's sake, but also because he genuinely believed something was awry in the Army – and he was part of the all-party group on Deepcut that was formed in the Commons. I really liked him, and his enthusiastic nature rubbed off on all the families. He was so full of fun and had a great sense of humour, and he kept us going, particularly during the difficult times. I had a chuckle to myself years later when I learned he was dating one of the Cheeky Girls: it was Lembit to a tee.

Lord Ashley of Stoke was another great asset to our campaign, this time within the House of Lords. He frequently raised the issue there and pushed for a public inquiry, despite being a Labour politician. Sadly, he died in April 2012. However, all the Deepcut families probably owe their biggest debt of gratitude to former Hull MP Kevin McNamara, who helped kick-start the whole campaign. In the early days when our appeals were falling on deaf ears, it was Kevin who brought the four families together, with the help of the BBC, and held that first press conference in June 2002. He and his parliamentary assistant Martin Collins also did vast amounts of research on Armed Forces deaths over the years, using much of it to form motions and parliamentary questions.

There was so much political goodwill towards us all at the local constituency level, with MPs on all sides demanding a public inquiry. However, it was a different story when it came to politicians at government level. Silence was golden, it seemed, when it came to Deepcut and Tony Blair's Labour administration.

We never once had any direct dealings with the prime minister, despite repeated attempts to lobby Downing Street. We wrote to Blair – and subsequently Gordon Brown and David Cameron after that – on numerous occasions and each time heard nothing. Indeed, the closest we ever came to Number 10 was in October 2004, when I got as far as the gates during a protest march with some of the other families from Deepcut and Beyond. The police allowed us to stand at the security barrier at the end of Downing Street and hand out leaflets before moving us on.

I was surprised by the silence from Blair, because he had promised so much when he took office in 1997. When we wrote to him, we tried to appeal to his human side as a father to young children, but all we ever got back was the same formal letter saying our correspondence had been passed on to the Defence Secretary, as the Prime Minister's Office had no jurisdiction over Army deaths.

Geoff Hoon, the Defence Secretary whose actions had prompted me to take to bed for months, was another who repeatedly blanked the Deepcut families. I did once try to speak with him face to face, when Diane Gray and I saw him walking across the main lobby at the House of Commons. If truth be told, it was more the case that we chased him across that floor as he tried to get away from us. His pace quickened and quickened as he attempted to brush us off and escape. However, the amusing thing was that as he darted through the front door he ended up walking straight into dozens of other bereaved parents from the Deepcut and Beyond group, who then proceeded to jostle him until he was rescued. I remember seeing a great photograph of that awkward moment on the BBC website hours later. That served him right: he should have spoken to me.

Adam Ingram, the Armed Forces Minister in Tony

Blair's cabinet, was a more affable man and was at least prepared to speak to, and meet with, the Deepcut families. Jim and I met him for the first time at the council offices in Perth in the spring of 2003. It was a very low-key meeting, and I think he only agreed to it in the first place because we assured him it would be away from cameras. There were only five of us in the room: Jim and me, Ingram and his assistant, and Annabelle Ewing. We outlined how the Army had treated us since James's death, and we asked for his thoughts about the allegations of bullying that were starting to emerge from Deepcut at that time. It wasn't long before the meeting got rather heated and we stopped for a break. Jim, Annabelle and Ingram's assistant stepped outside for fresh air, leaving the Minister and myself in the room. With no one else around, I had to take the opportunity that presented itself, so I asked him, one on one, why he couldn't back a public inquiry.

'Although you don't have children of your own, perhaps you have nieces or nephews?' I said to him. 'Surely you would want to find out what had happened to them if it was a member of your immediate family? I'm sure you have a heart. Why won't you help ease our pain and hold a public inquiry?'

He paused and thought for a second. 'I was very close to calling an inquiry,' he confessed. 'But I can't. It would bring the Army into disrepute and it is already affecting recruitment figures. We can't make the situation any worse.'

I appreciated his honesty, but I couldn't understand why he didn't want to remedy the problem, rather than walking away from it. I told him I wasn't anti-Army, expressed my admiration for our soldiers, and suggested to him that a public inquiry that found a solution and brought an end to the scandal would restore faith in the

Armed Forces and help drive recruitment figures back up. Ingram was having none of it, but I got the impression he felt stuck between a rock and a hard place. There were signs that he did sympathise with us and thought we deserved a public inquiry to get the answers we craved, but he was duty bound by his job. Unlike many government officials we encountered, I quite liked him and could tell that he had a human side but had been placed in a difficult position.

We met Ingram again about a year after that, this time in London ahead of his announcing an independent review of the Deepcut deaths – about which more to come later. He had arranged the meeting as a courtesy to let us know before it was made public that Nicholas Blake, a highly respected QC, had been given a wide scope to look into the barracks. On one hand, Ingram had been decent enough to tell us about the decision in advance – unlike Geoff Hoon months earlier when he had ruled out a public inquiry live on television – but on the other, I saw it as a cop-out. If the government was concerned enough about Deepcut to go to the trouble of sanctioning an independent review, why not just hold a public inquiry? It didn't make a lot of sense.

Ingram was the only member of the Labour cabinet who ever took the time to meet with us. His successor as Armed Forces Minister, Bob Ainsworth, sent us a few formal letters to update us on certain matters, but that was it. We did try to contact the likes of John Reid and Jim Murphy, both Scots who held the Defence portfolio after Geoff Hoon, without getting very far. Each letter we did receive contained the same rhetoric and repeatedly told us a public inquiry was not required. Without fail, every single piece of correspondence from the Ministry of Defence said exactly the same thing: 'There is no evidence of collusion, cover-up, breach of legal duty of care or any other failure to foresee or prevent any individual death. There is no credible evidence that any of the four deaths was prompted by bullying or harassment. It is important that we do now move forward. I can assure you that the Ministry of Defence is determined to do everything it can to learn lessons from these sad events and give young recruits the care and support that they and their parents have a right to expect.' Yawn.

We didn't see any point in writing to royalty; after all, it was a government matter and we knew any letters we sent to Buckingham Palace would only be passed on to the relevant minister for action – and then be binned.

We never lobbied Holyrood either, and we stayed away from involving Members of the Scottish Parliament (MSPs) because we knew only Westminster had jurisdiction over the Armed Forces and matters of UK national defence. James had also died at a barracks in England, so no fatal accident inquiry – the Scottish equivalent of a coroner's inquest – could be held in Scotland. The Scottish National Party (SNP) took a particular interest in the campaign and backed our demands for a public inquiry, but with only a handful of MPs in the Commons, there was very little they could do to influence Westminster. That said, the Scottish government is looking to bring in new legislation that would allow inquiries to be held into sudden and unexplained deaths of Scots outwith Scottish soil. There is even speculation that the remit could be extended to include deaths that have already taken place. Whether this would give any scope for James's case to be looked at, I don't know, but it is something we would obviously embrace if it was possible. When you are desperate for answers after so many years, you will try any avenue.

The one avenue I would never go down, however, is standing for parliament myself: even if it was the only way

I could secure a public inquiry. It is becoming common-place for ordinary people to stand for election on the back of a campaign or single issue, more often than not against a high-profile cabinet minister. It's not something I would ever consider, though. Yvonne Collinson Heath MP? I think not.

17. The Coroner's Inquest

We had been without James in our lives for three years, ten months and twenty-eight days by the time the official inquest into his death was finally convened. It had been a long wait, that's for sure. Having been provisionally arranged for early in 2003, it had been delayed until the police investigation was over. It was now 20 February 2006.

I was apprehensive about the coroner's inquest, because it would bring to the fore all the painful memories and all the hurt I had managed to suppress for so long. The purpose of these inquests is to outline the circumstances in which a person has died, and for us, it meant being able to hear for the first time many of the details about what happened to James in his last few hours at the barracks. I desperately wanted to hear these, but, at the same time, I wasn't sure whether or not I would actually be able to cope with it all. My stomach was in knots for days leading up to the inquest opening. I knew it would be difficult to listen to at times, but we had to focus on the bigger picture and hope that the outcome could be used to force a public inquiry.

Since March 2002, we had learned very little about James's death or the hours leading up to the shooting. We hadn't met many of his former colleagues at the barracks, and we certainly hadn't come face to face with any of the officers responsible for him. At the very least, I wanted the inquest to fill in these gaps about his life at Deepcut, and satisfy me that he hadn't been at the centre of the bullying and sexual harassment that now seemed to have been so rampant.

We were aware that the man due to preside over the inquest was Michael Burgess, a high-profile figure who was, and still is, the Coroner of the Queen's Household. He was particularly well known at the time of James's inquest because he was rarely out of the news: he was also preparing to take charge of the inquiry into the death of Diana, Princess of Wales, due to be held later that year. He was more than qualified to be hearing the inquest into James's death. Mr Burgess had already taken charge of the inquests into the three other Deepcut deaths and was very familiar with the case. However, we were told James's inquest would run differently to that of Geoff Gray four years earlier. For starters, it was expected to last at least a month – compared to a matter of hours for the Grays – and as the case was deemed to be of public interest, we were given legal aid so we could instruct a solicitor and a barrister to act on our behalf and question witnesses, while a jury would also be in place to decide on the verdict. It wasn't a surprise, given the media attention in Deepcut since 2002.

The day before the inquest opened at Epsom Magistrates' Court, Jim and I travelled together from Perth to Surrey. We chatted about what we expected to learn, what the potential outcome might be and what questions we would like to be asked of certain witnesses. We had been given a lever arch file of witness statements and a timetable of events for the coming weeks. When we arrived in Epsom, we checked into the hotel Surrey Police had arranged for us before being taken to the court by the family liaison officers for a private meeting with Mr Burgess. He was very welcoming and guided us through how proceedings would unfold, and he confessed that he had long felt there should be some kind of inquiry into the four Deepcut deaths. That really put us at ease and took away much of the anxiety I was feeling.

The next morning, the tension in the hushed courtroom was unbearable as we sat waiting for the coroner to arrive to formally open the inquest. You could cut the atmosphere with a knife, and, with every set of eyes on me and Jim as the bereaved parents, in many ways I felt as if I was about to be placed on trial for having committed a crime. Geoff and Diane were in the public gallery, sat directly behind us for moral support, while near us were four sets of legal teams: one for us, one for the Army, one for the police and a fourth for the two privates who had been with James on the night he died. The Army lawyers sat directly in front of us, and I have to say they looked, and felt like, the opposition. Not once did they exchange any pleasantries with us; not once did they even bother to shake our hands. Behind us in the public gallery, reading a newspaper, was Lt Col. Ron Laden, the commanding officer of Deepcut. He was the eyes at the back of the room.

The first to give evidence was the coroner's officer I had met at the mortuary in 2002 when I had identified James's body. I had been so full of hope when proceedings began, but her testimony really set the tone for how the rest of the inquest would pan out. For starters, the inquest simply glossed over one of the more harrowing moments of my visit to see James's body. I will never forget the final words from the coroner's officer before Malcolm and I headed in to face our worst nightmare on that morning back in 2002.

'Oh, there is one more thing you need to know before you go through,' the coroner's officer had said as we headed for the door. 'I have a little bit of good news. As part of the post-mortem, we checked James for any signs of homosexuality and you'll be pleased to know there were none.'

I was bemused at the time. I didn't have any idea what she was talking about. Was she telling me I would be glad to know my son wasn't gay? I didn't care if James was gay or bisexual; it never really mattered to us. What did his sexuality have to do with any of this? How could it be of any relevance? Looking back on it now, I often think about what this woman said to us. With the benefit of hindsight, I think what was being implied was that there was no sign of James having been raped or sexually assaulted. At the time I was dumbfounded and slightly hurt by what she said, if truth be told, yet it barely warranted a mention at the coroner's inquest. The woman said she didn't say it, and that was accepted, yet why would I make such a thing up?

Next was Dr David Rouse, the Home Office pathologist who had carried out the second post-mortem on James in October 2002. Despite our hopes being raised at the time, he told the jury James had died instantly from a self-inflicted, close-range gunshot wound to the head. He also said there was no evidence to suggest the gun had been forced into his hand, or that he had been assaulted. Dr Rouse concluded by saying that the soot patterns under James's chin were consistent with suicide, as was the angle of the bullet: the opposite to what Frank Swann had told the families three years earlier. It wasn't the best start to the proceedings.

The second and third days weren't much better. When asked to recall the scene of the shooting and the position of the gun in relation to James's body, both a police officer and an Army investigator gave different accounts to the ones they had given in 2002. They hadn't taken adequate notes at the time of the shooting, and their recollections weren't what they were. I was starting to doubt if we would get a clearer picture of what had happened to James.

After them came two soldiers who gave evidence claiming James had made a remark, on two separate occasions, that he was going to kill himself. Private Michael Foody told the jury he had been in the guardroom when James walked in and made the comment, but dismissed it because he knew James was 'a jokey person'. The BBC report of the evidence that day notes that Private Foody said, 'If I knew he was serious I would have gone and told someone but I thought he was just joking around. I thought he was just being his normal self.' Lance Corporal Scott Smith gave a similar account to the jury and said he had been on a minibus taking the soldiers to the guard postings when he heard James say, 'Just you wait until I get a rifle. I will kill myself.'

What they said surprised many people, but we had known it was coming, because Surrey Police had informed us. However, we found the soldiers' evidence difficult to believe, because it had taken these two soldiers many months to come forward with this supposed information in the first place. If James truly had said he was going to shoot himself moments before he was found dead – and was subsequently found with a bullet hole in his head – then surely two of the last people to see him alive would have immediately reported that? Yet they didn't. I know James, and I don't believe he said that.

Lance Corporal Smith also told the jury that my son was not popular within Deepcut, but anyone we had ever spoken with privately had said the opposite. One witness even gave evidence saying that he had spent the final Friday evening in James's company, yet I knew James had been with me at home that night. It just wasn't true. I wondered if these soldiers even knew who James was. He'd only been there six weeks and they may have got him confused with another soldier.

A week into the inquest came evidence that James had been given the gun that killed him by one of the two other soldiers on guard duty. There had been three of them doing the gruelling two-hours-on, two-hours-off shift: James and Privates John Donnelly and Stacy McGrath. The jury was told what we already knew: that James was too young to have a gun and instead wore a fluorescent vest and carried a torch, while the other two men were armed with SA-80 rifles. Private Donnelly said that James wanted to go off into the bushes for a cigarette and asked to borrow his gun. Smoking on guard duty was strictly prohibited, and apparently James felt that bearing a firearm would make it look less like he was bunking off from his post if he happened to be caught in the shrubbery by an officer. Moments later, a single gunshot rang out, and James was dead.

All I could think of when Private Donnelly was giving his evidence were James's words just hours before he died. He told me soldiers were not allowed to wander off on their own, never mind with a loaded weapon. Even going for a comfort break would lead to a recruit having a chaperone, James had said. Yet here was the last person to have seen him alive claiming James had done exactly that: asked for the gun and walked off alone. How could that be?

The inquest heard that Private McGrath had been on the phone to his girlfriend during the guard duty – against Deepcut rules – and had turned his back as Private Donnelly handed over his weapon to James. He said he had returned to his post to find that the other two soldiers had swapped roles, with Private Donnelly sporting the high-visibility vest and the torch and James now somewhere out of view with the rifle.

When the shot rang out, the soldiers said they took no action because they weren't certain it had been a gun.

According to the *Daily Mail* report of the hearing the next day, Private McGrath told the jury, 'Between five and ten minutes of me and John talking we heard what appeared to be a single gunshot, which seemed close at the time.

'I possibly presumed it was going to be the ranges but there are no ranges firing at night. I thought it was some kind of firework or pyrotechnic coming from the Officers' Mess at the time, a rocket going off.'

He went on to explain that he and Private Donnelly waited for a while before deciding to go looking for James. McGrath went to search first, but came back after a few minutes to say he couldn't find him. However, he later admitted he didn't actually look for him because he was afraid, having heard the gunshot. Private Donnelly then went off to search and subsequently found James's body, before contacting the guardroom. His message was received by a female private who jotted down the conversation on a notepad in front of her. In her evidence, she stated that when she went back to the same pad to make a formal version of what had been said, her notes had already been mysteriously rewritten by someone else, and her original scrawling was never seen again.

Our barrister, John Cooper QC, grilled the two male soldiers for quite some time on their version of events and even put it to them that perhaps they had stood under James and fired the gun through his chin. They were asked repeatedly if they killed James. 'No sir, no sir,' came their reply.

I felt sorry for Private Donnelly in the end. No matter how James met his death, it must have been a traumatic experience for him, because he had, apparently, found the body. It was also Private Donnelly who had made the emergency radio call to the guardroom saying, 'Zero Zero, man down, man down. He's still twitching.' He must have been on the scene fairly quickly to have seen James still moving, because the medical consensus is that he died instantly – yet in his evidence he said they had waited a while before looking for him. There were so many contradictions. According to evidence from another soldier later in the inquest, Private Donnelly was found crying shortly after the shooting. 'I should never have given him the gun,' he was sobbing.

The girl James had been dating when he died also gave evidence at the hearing. Her name was Kelly, but I didn't know a great deal about her because the relationship had been fairly new, so much so that I didn't even meet her for the first time until the day of the inquest. She spoke very highly of James and said that the pair had arranged to meet up once the guard duty shift was over, telling the jury that he was his normal self and in a good state of mind. Kelly also said that just as he was about to get on the minibus taking him to his guard post at the Officers' Mess, James had said, 'I have something to tell you.' He didn't get the chance to say it, though, because he was ordered onto the bus by a sergeant, and she was never to find out what news he had for her.

Gruesome details about how and where James had been found were made public for the first time at the inquest, giving us a clearer picture of what faced those arriving on the scene that fateful night. James had been lying on his back close to the perimeter fence with his legs outstretched. His left arm was down the side of his body while his right arm was across his chest with his finger still over the trigger of the gun, which was pointing down towards his feet. There was an entry wound under his chin and an exit wound at the top of his head towards his right ear. It was so large that the top of his skull had been blown off and his brain matter was down by his feet, where it had landed following the blast. One paramedic told how he had to crawl about in the dark looking for other bits of James's brain.

Much of this Jim and I knew already, but it was still hard to listen to, and it clearly came as quite a shock to the men and women of the jury. They were visibly upset, but that wasn't a surprise given the nature of what was being outlined to them. Worse still, the jury also had to endure seeing photographs of the gunshot wound. I had never seen them before – and didn't want to see them – but unfortunately caught a glimpse of one during a witness testimony. Hearing the gruesome details of your son's death is one thing; seeing an image of him lying there with his brains blown out is another. It will live with me for ever.

It was very tough having the ins and outs of James's life, and his death, played out in public for three weeks. The hardest part for me wasn't hearing about his final moments at the camp, but telling the jury about his last hours with me at home. I told them how I wished I could press the rewind button and turn back the clock. The jurors asked me questions directly – which was something I was surprised to learn can happen in a coroner's court – and I could tell from the things they asked that they were sympathetic to my feelings.

The Army lawyers weren't the least bit sympathetic towards me, however, and there were times I felt as if I was being interrogated, as if somehow I was to blame for my own son's death. They painted a picture of James being unruly, having money problems and being distraught about his dad and me splitting up. It was nonsense, as far as I was concerned, but I couldn't help but worry that I was being judged by the jury. What if they thought I was to blame, that I was a terrible mother?

As part of the proceedings, we were all taken on a day trip to Deepcut. The jurors were taken on a walk of the perimeter fence as James's final steps were retraced, and, as I watched from a distance, I could see they were trying to picture the scene in their minds. When they had moved on, Jim and I went to the spot and placed a rose. The guided tour carried on to the guardroom, where I noticed a number of posters on the wall informing recruits that bullying would not be tolerated. I bet they weren't there in 2002! Our final stop was the firing range, where everyone was shown how an SA-80 rifle worked. The noise was incredible, and the sound of bullets echoed around us for what seemed like for ever. I could feel the sound vibrate in my head. It was a distressing moment for me, because all I could think of was James. That bang, that cacophony, was the last thing he ever heard.

There were positives from the inquest: we heard how well James was doing at Deepcut and how highly regarded he was by his peers. We were told he was regularly being praised and appeared to have overcome any difficulties he might have had as a result of his dyslexia. The jury was also shown a letter James had written to the learning support teacher he'd had at school. He was proud of himself and had wanted to say thanks for all the help he had received that had given him the chance to join the Army. Our barrister showed this letter to a psychologist, appearing as a witness for Surrey Police, who then bizarrely said it indicated James might not have been in a sound state of mind and was unhappy with Army life. Rather than agreeing it was a positive note to a former teacher, she pointed out the spelling mistakes and bad handwriting of someone suffering from dyslexia. We couldn't win.

It was also nice hearing some of the stories about his life at the barracks. For example, we learned that when he turned up for that fateful final guard duty James was given a light-hearted telling off because he was fidgeting. He couldn't help it, though: he'd heard the strains of bagpipes coming from elsewhere in the barracks and couldn't keep still. He was a proud Scot to the last.

As the days passed, the various inadequacies and

failures of the Surrey Police investigation were outlined to the jury. I had to stifle a laugh at the evidence from one forensic expert brought in by detectives to replicate the circumstances of the gunshot wound. He told the jury that he had used a bag of cotton wool, with an Army cap placed on top, to act as a human head. Cotton wool! Even without having any scientific expertise myself, I had to question whether this could possibly produce accurate results, and I caught the eye of one of the jurors, who sat there shaking his head in disbelief. It was Frank Swann all over again.

When the last of the witnesses had given their evidence, I wasn't sure what the jury would decide. Some of the testimonies clearly suggested James had killed himself, but some of them had pointed towards something else. Before the inquest began, we were hopeful that a verdict of unlawful killing would be recorded, but the coroner ruled out that option when directing the jury. Summing up, he told them there was no evidence of a scuffle or disturbance around the body, nor was there anything to suggest that Privates McGrath or Donnelly had murdered James. Instead, Mr Burgess directed the jury to choose between suicide and accidental death, or record an open verdict. That was a disappointment, but then again there hadn't been any evidence to show James had been murdered. The next-best option for us was the open verdict, because it meant we could continue to push for a public inquiry since there would still be so many unanswered questions surrounding James's death.

The tension in the court was even more unbearable than it had been at the very beginning of the proceedings, and I could barely stand the air of anticipation as the jury filed back into their seats. My fingers tingled and my heart felt as if it was beating so fast it would explode out of my chest. An eternity seemed to pass before anyone spoke, but then we heard the two words we so desperately wanted to hear: 'Open verdict.' It was such a relief, and I let out a sigh so loud that many people in the courtroom turned to see where it had come from. We were in tears; some of the jurors were in tears. It was the end to one of the biggest emotional roller coasters of my life.

In his final address, the coroner was true to the promise he made to us at the start of proceedings and said he believed that some form of inquiry into the Deepcut deaths should be held. He said, 'My own personal view – and I emphasise that it is a personal view – is that the MoD should take whatever steps are necessary to restore public confidence in the recruitment and training of young soldiers whether at Deepcut or elsewhere.

'I personally believe that they should have nothing to fear from an inquiry held in public . . . where the various issues . . . can be explored in greater depth.'

Mr Burgess also vowed to write to the Defence Secretary highlighting his concerns on a number of issues – such as the way weapons are handed out and how emergencies are dealt with by Army officials – and said that 'there has to be some way of resolving the unease there seems to be about Deepcut'. His remarks gave us exactly what we needed to carry on our fight.

While very little had happened over the course of the previous year ahead of the inquest opening, we did receive a boost in March 2005 when the Army was criticised by the Commons Defence Select Committee in its final report into Deepcut. More than 120 recommendations pertaining to standards of care within the barracks, and the Armed Forces in general, were made by MPs. Among the suggestions were that the Ministry of Defence should consider raising the minimum age of recruits from 16 to 18, and ban soldiers under 18 from having to undertake guard duty. The report called for changes in the way training was conducted and urged the Army to change the way it characterised victims as 'weak' and discouraged complaint. It also recommended the creation of an independent complaints commission and called for a 'change of culture' to allow the MoD to 'bear down on the bullies'.

The committee also said that the level of support given to the families of soldiers killed in non-combat circumstances 'fell well short' of that given to those who had died, as heroes, in action. All in all, it was a damning critique of the British Armed Forces as they stood in 2005.

Surrey Police had fared no better when an interim report into the force's handling of the Deepcut investigations was released by Devon and Cornwall Police in November 2005. It criticised the mindset of officers, said they failed to follow leads and noted that detectives decided too quickly the deaths had all been suicides. The review concluded that there had been a 'lack of focus' and guidelines 'were not followed'. It came as no great surprise to us.

By the spring of 2006, two years had passed since the day Geoff Hoon had ruled out a public inquiry. With the coroner's inquest over, we still felt there was enough new evidence, enough new doubt about Deepcut, for the government to perform a U-turn. Yes, it felt as if we were going two steps forward, one step back, but this time it looked as if we were at last edging closer to the truth.

18. Time for a Step Back

It only took 19 days for us to come crashing back down to earth following the high of the inquest. Having spent fifteen months examining the Deepcut controversy, and the four deaths in particular, Nicholas Blake QC published his findings on 29 March 2006. They did not make for good reading.

All four families were invited to meet Mr Blake at Canary Wharf in London to discuss his review ahead of it being made public. I remember that morning well, as we sat there taking in the view of some of London's famous landmarks from a bird's-eye view. As we anxiously waited around a long conference table, he walked into the room, dropped a copy of the report in front of each of us and then announced he hadn't backed our calls for a public inquiry. He sat down at the table for a few minutes and tried to explain that he hadn't deemed such a move necessary, but Des James interrupted him. Des looked Mr Blake in the eyes and said, 'You've finished us. You know that, don't you?' The QC shrugged his shoulders and promptly left us to it.

At more than 500 pages long, *The Deepcut Review* was quite weighty and made a bit of a thump on the table. We then had about 30 minutes to digest what was contained inside before Blake held a press conference with Surrey

Police at the other side of London and the long-awaited document was made public.

Why we were told to meet at Canary Wharf we do not know, but we can only imagine it was an attempt to keep the Deepcut families away from where the media had assembled. It was an impossible task trying to read all the pages in time, so each family started by sifting through the section relating to our own child. What we found broke our hearts: Blake had concluded that the four soldiers killed themselves and, as he had already announced, that no public inquiry should be held.

As we skim read the *Review*, we discovered he had also decided that:

- There was no evidence Sean Benton had been bullied, and his death was not caused by the negligence or breach of duty by the Army;
- There was no reliable evidence Cheryl James had been the victim of sexual harassment, and her death was most likely as a result of complications in her private life;
- Neither the Army nor any other soldier was to blame for what happened to Geoff Gray; and
- A number of unfortunate circumstances came together, leading to James being able to take his own life.

We were devastated. Nicholas Blake had promised us so much, but, like everyone else before him, delivered nothing. He had built us up, dropping subtle hints that he would back a public inquiry, and we had put more faith and trust in him than we ever had with anyone else. Ultimately, it did us no good and we felt cheated. It came as the biggest blow to the families in four years, and Des James, in particular, was a broken man. I had never seen him so low, and it worried me.

We managed to find out where Blake had gone for the

press conference and decided to race across London after him, huffing and puffing with that weighty report under our arms, to gatecrash the announcement. As far as we were concerned, we should not have been excluded from that gathering in the first place, but we arrived just as it came to an end. The afternoon gave us time to read Blake's conclusions in more depth, but what we found out about our loved ones made us even more distraught.

Blake concluded that Sean Benton had been nothing more than a troubled individual who had shot himself, and made a great deal about how a difficult upbringing had influenced his Army career, as if trying to prove his point. He made public for the first time the fact that Sean had taken a paracetamol overdose at the age of sixteen, some three years before he even enlisted for the Army, and noted that Social Services and Child Guidance Services had been required during this same period in his life. When Sean signed up in 1994 and reported to Pirbright for his Phase 1 training, he struggled, and the *Review* included statements from officers to the effect that they believed he would never make a good soldier. The report said that by the time Sean had moved on to Phase 2 at Deepcut he had become 'emotionally unstable and prone to crying and abuse of alcohol'. He had also failed his driver training twice and was facing a less prestigious Army career as a pioneer, a soldier who performs basic construction work.

The Deepcut Review noted that on 7 February 1995, Sean had injured himself with a door window he had deliberately broken while drunk and had threatened suicide. He was treated at the medical centre and then seen by a psychiatrist, who concluded that while he had temperament issues, he did not have any psychiatric problems. On 14 February, Sean was fined £100 and punished with a seven-day restriction on privileges after swearing at a commanding officer. He got in trouble again just a week later and needed

213

medical treatment once more after kicking in a window at the accommodation block. On 12 April, Sean was rushed to accident and emergency after taking 22 Anadin tablets, with a subsequent psychiatric report noting that he was deeply unhappy at the barracks, was suffering financial problems, and was jealous that his friends had progressed as drivers and he had not. Things didn't get any better for him, and he was told he would be discharged from the Army after an incident in a pub on 1 June during which he swore at a female NCO, and threatened to shoot her if he was put on guard duty again. It was only seven days later that Sean was found dead.

In his report, Blake painted a bleak picture of Sean Benton's days at the barracks, and they were bleak, but he didn't fully explain why. We had heard so many accounts of his having been bullied – bullied to death, as one BBC documentary speculated – yet the *Review* simply glossed over this. Eight pages in the report were dedicated to claims of horrific physical and psychological abuse suffered by Sean, including alleged instances of his being severely beaten and kicked in the kidney region by one NCO, or being humiliated in front of the other recruits. However, Blake said that 'there is no consistent and reliable evidence that over-harsh discipline caused him to become depressed'. He added that there was 'no evidence that Sean had been bullied shortly before his death or that he had ever complained of bullying to his close friends or anyone in authority'. Instead, pointing clearly towards suicide and no third-party involvement, Blake ended, 'Sean Benton was known to have become emotionally distressed and had engaged in at least two attempts at self-harm in the months before he died. The conclusion of the *Review* is that he was neither bullied to death nor was his death caused by the negligence or breach of duty of the Army.'

It was devastating for the Bentons. While they probably

believed, deep down, that their son had killed himself, they had been desperate to prove that someone was to blame for driving him to the brink. It wasn't to be.

Blake painted a different picture of life at Deepcut for Cheryl James, with the *Review* noting she was a good recruit, progressed quickly through her training and was well liked by fellow soldiers. However, he concluded that she too had shot herself, and in assessing the circumstances leading up to her death, he determined that 'complications in her private life' were the biggest factor. She had been having a relationship with two different soldiers, and on 25 November 1995, just two days before she died, Cheryl was found in bed with another private by her boyfriend. The *Review* included a statement from one of her friends, who had told Blake that Cheryl 'could not make up her mind' between the two soldiers.

On the morning of her death, Cheryl had reported for guard duty at 6.30 a.m. and was assigned to do the stag on her own, against Army regulations, at Royal Way Gate, a quiet barrier open only at selected times to allow officers to enter. A handful of people are on record as having seen her during the first 90 minutes of her shift, including her new love interest, who met her at the gate at 7.30 a.m. and spoke with her for 45 minutes until being asked to leave by a major. About five minutes later, a senior officer arriving at the gate noticed it was unmanned, and the matter was raised with the guardroom at 8.30 a.m. When a lance corporal came to investigate, he noticed a camouflage jacket in the wooded area next to the gate and discovered Cheryl's body. She had a large wound to the front of her head and her SA-80 was lying by her side.

Over the years, we had heard allegations that Cheryl had been the subject of sexual propositioning by a corporal at Leconfield, and it was something that had hurt her parents deeply. However, Blake concluded that there was 'no evidence' of this and said it might have been nothing more than a rumour. He added, 'This Review does not believe that if Cheryl was sexually propositioned by a Corporal . . . that this was a lasting concern affecting her state of mind by 27 November.'

Blake also added that 'there is no evidence that bullying was a factor in her death' and instead concluded she had shot herself because of 'personal factors during a period of unresolved complications in her private life, at a time when she may have been vulnerable and lacking in self-esteem'. He continued, 'Taken together, and alongside what is known of Cheryl's activities over the weekend, a picture of a period of tiring activity and little sleep, combined with emotional turmoil emerges.'

In other words: 'one bullet, one body, draw your own conclusion'. We had heard it all before, but it didn't make his report any less painful to read. For the Grays, *The Deepcut Review* was particularly difficult to take in, because they felt the facts surrounding their own son's death had been presented in such a way to make it look like a suicide.

When he had signed up to the Army in January 2001, Geoff Gray had always dreamed of becoming a soldier. A former Scout, he wrote on his application form that he saw a military career as 'a new experience, giving me a challenge and a chance to learn new skills'. He added, 'I always work my best and like to be pushed to new extremes both physically and mentally. I think the Army will help build myself to a new person teaching me many new things.'

Like James, he was posted to Pirbright for Phase 1 training, but with a view to becoming a supply controller in the Royal Logistic Corps. He passed out in April 2001 and earned good reports from his troop commander, who described him as 'a hard worker' and said 'he tries hard in all lessons and has shown no difficulties throughout'.

When he was posted to Deepcut for Phase 2 training, it was clear that Geoff, again like James, despised guard duty. The *Review* noted that on the night he died, Geoff was supposedly overheard by another private saying he was intending to shoot himself. Recalling an interview with that private, the report stated, 'Geoff said, "Guard is really depressing . . . I've done two twenty-four hour shifts in the weekend. I feel like shooting myself."' Another trainee on the stag that night recounted a similar conversation with Geoff and claimed he had said, 'I wonder what it is like being shot in the head.'

The *Review* said that Geoff bore the brunt of teasing during one of the rest breaks that night after he confessed to a sexual relationship with a deaf woman. It noted that 'after some initial bravado about this incident, Geoff may have become ashamed of his actions once he became the subject of further teasing'. Shortly after 1.15 a.m., Geoff told a female colleague he was going to do a 'prowler patrol': essentially a foot patrol of the area. He had been assigned a weapon – against Army rules, because he was still only 17 – and went off on his own. Between three to five minutes later, the female private heard a burst of shots. Geoff was dead.

In his conclusion, Blake said the death of Geoff Gray was 'perplexing' and that it was 'very difficult to understand why a healthy, enthusiastic and popular young man . . . should want to turn his weapon on himself and fire it'. However, he added that it was 'even more perplexing' why anyone would want to ambush him alone during guard duty and shoot him from close range. Instead, like the other deaths, Blake suggested that 'despite outward appearances, he was a serious minded young man with some personal issues to face in his private life'.

In the years following Geoff's death, his parents had

raised repeated questions about the length of time it took to find his body and also about more recent claims that a private had witnessed someone sprinting across a field after the gunshot went off. Blake, however, concluded that the soldiers conducting the search on the night were 'in an understandably emotive and anxious state' and had misinterpreted shadows and noises in the grounds. He pointed to the fact that there were no breaks in the perimeter fence, said no footprints were found on the dewy grass near the body to suggest anyone had run away, and insisted that Geoff's body had only been missed because it was lying at the foot of a small mound. The Grays were gutted; it really knocked them for six.

There was very little in *The Deepcut Review* about James, because Blake had been wary about examining his death since the coroner was also investigating and at that point the inquest hadn't yet been held. However, Blake did speculate that James might still have been alive today had several Army regulations not been breached on the night he died. The soldier who had handed over his gun to James had broken the rules, the other recruit who was on his mobile phone to his girlfriend during guard duty had broken the rules, and James wandering away for a smoke was against the rules, as was insisting he was going off alone. All of this, the *Review* noted, came together to create a window of opportunity for a shooting to take place. It sounded a plausible theory, but it's something we'll not be able to prove either way.

No soldier was ever subsequently charged with breaking any of these rules, and when I queried this, all I was told was that my James had been just as guilty as the others, and he couldn't be charged, so why punish them? I couldn't help but think that the loss of his life was punishment enough.

While Blake concluded the four deaths were suicides,

his decision not to back a public inquiry was still surprising, because his report also provided the most shocking insights to date about the brutality of the regime at Deepcut. Dozens of pages were dedicated to horrific incidents of sexual abuse, bullying and degrading treatment, the majority of which was carried out by senior officers on new recruits.

He told of one sergeant in particular, who recruits said had a split personality and would threaten to bring out his imaginary 'twin' to hand out punishment. Trainees told how he would also hide in long grass and spring out at them, discipline them with endless parades for no reason, or force them to do sit-ups in the mud just because he was bored. One recruit told the *Review* the sergeant was 'extremely strict and seemed mad' and added, 'He used to say he was going to get his brother then turn around shouting and spitting at us. It was his threat of "shall I go and get my brother?"' Another soldier said the officer was 'the most evil person one could imagine'.

Former recruits told the *Review* how senior NCOs would offer inducements such as less guard duty or less menial tasks in return for sexual favours, with sex being viewed as 'a passport for getting off all sorts of things'. Another sergeant major allegedly encouraged privates to attack trainees with a bar of soap inside a sock if they were letting the squadron down.

The *Review* also found that alcohol was a major problem at Deepcut, with one soldier telling Blake that the camp was 'out of control'. He added, 'After working hours it was just like Glasgow or London on a Saturday night. This was every night. For example at the disco at the NAAFI midweek recruits were completely drunk. Both sexes. Staff would be needed to stop fights.'

It seemed astonishing that on one hand Blake had uncovered a catalogue of abuse, then on the other hand for his report to say the four deaths were not connected to any of this. Sean Benton, Cheryl James, Geoff Gray and my son all just chose to take their own lives, but it was nothing to do with the camp from hell? It sounded implausible.

The *Review* also outlined, for the first time, how dilapidated the Princess Royal Barracks was, with soldiers forced to live in almost squalid conditions. Blake noted that the camp was built in the 1960s and that each dorm contained eight beds, with privacy and security a problem for recruits. Washrooms were communal, plumbing regularly broke down, toilets often became blocked and the camp was 'in need of modernising and updating'. Painting a bleak picture – perhaps in a further bid to show why our loved ones might have taken their own lives – Blake also noted that there had been forty-seven suicide attempts in little more than three years.

The government's official response to the *Review* three months later was, unsurprisingly, equally dismissive of the Deepcut families. For the second time in as many years, Geoff Hoon acknowledged that mistakes had been made in the handling of the deaths, and that there were deficiencies in the Army's system of care, but he stuck by his original decision not to hold a public inquiry. His short 16-page report was another whitewash as far as we were concerned.

In his conclusions, Blake had made 20 recommendations for urgent action to be taken by the Ministry of Defence – such as increasing the ratio of instructors to recruits in training camps, and ensuring soldiers had reached the age of 18 before being posted to units – but on almost every occasion, Hoon said the Army was already in the process of remedying the situation. There was no case to answer, in other words.

It's fair to say the families were at our lowest ebb by

this stage. Blake had been our last hope, and it felt like the end as far as the campaign was concerned. As the Deepcut Four we had been banging our heads against a brick wall for exactly four years, and there was nowhere else for us to turn. We were all tired, and we had to let it go. Even Harry Benton, who rarely gave any comments to the media, told the BBC that 'the time has come where we draw a line under it all'.

With the latest defeat came the dawning realisation that four years had passed and that I had pushed friends and family aside in the desperate attempt to find out what had happened to James. Stuart, Claire, Malcolm and the boys: they had all been neglected, and as much as they seemed outwardly not to mind, I knew inside they ached and craved my love. I had to remind myself that life was for the living, not the dead.

The truth was, I hadn't been a proper mother to Stuart and Claire since 2002, and their lives were passing me by. A mother is supposed to be there supporting her children, and in the days after James died, Stuart was at a critical time in his academic career, yet I didn't even know what exams he was sitting. As for Claire, she was still a little girl when she lost her brother but had now been through puberty and was going to secondary school, and I hadn't been there to answer her questions about growing up. On days that I was off campaigning, I would ask neighbours to look after the children, or they would be farmed out to other family members. During the times I was actually at home, it was common for Stuart and Claire to finish school and find that the living room had been taken over by journalists and camera crews. The sad thing is that I never noticed; I didn't realise that I was slowly drifting apart from my own family. Like a horse with blinkers on, all I cared about was Deepcut and getting justice for my James.

Life couldn't have been easy for Stuart and Claire; I

realise that now. First of all they had to cope with their parents' separation, then they lost their brother, and finally they had to deal with growing up without the proper love and support of their mother and father. Claire needed to have a counsellor at school, while Stuart became quite insular. How they managed, I do not know, and I will always regret the fact I wasn't there for them.

After Blake's *Review* was published, I made sure I spent more time with the people I cared about most, and I enjoyed rebuilding my relationship with Stuart and Claire in particular. The arrival of Stuart's first child at about this time helped bring me back to reality. Little Joshua James Collinson had been born while Jim and I attended the coroner's inquest in Epsom, and with the campaign now on the back burner we had an opportunity to enjoy our new roles as grandparents. I had already missed out on my children growing up and did not want the same to happen with my grandchildren. And, as difficult a decision as it was to make, I had to leave Deepcut to one side. I couldn't go on any longer. It was time to take a step back.

19. True Happiness

The English actress and author Nanette Newman once famously said, 'A good marriage is at least 80 per cent good luck in finding the right person at the right time. The rest is trust.' She could have been talking about me. On 24 July 2007, I tied the knot with Malcolm, the man who most certainly had come into my life at the right time. More than six years had passed since we had first met, and he truly was the love of my life: my soulmate.

It's fair to say our wedding, at Gretna Green registry office, was a quiet affair. We had both been married before: Malcolm's first marriage didn't work out and ended in divorce after three years. We dressed in casual attire – Malcolm sported a shirt and tie, and I wore a long pink skirt with a white top, and even used my corsage as an impromptu bouquet – and we didn't have any fancy limousines or anything like that. We literally turned up in our own car, and then waited in the car park outside for my brother and his wife, who were to be our witnesses. They had picked up some flowers from a florist in Ellesmere Port on their way north to Scotland, and so there we were, the four of us standing outside the registry office trying every which way to get a flower to remain in place in my hair, in order for me to look at least a little like the blushing bride.

We chose Gretna because it was about halfway between Perth, where we still lived, and Ellesmere Port, where my dad and his wife, as well as my brother and his family, stayed in England. In fact, when we originally planned the wedding we were simply going to drive down and visit them but stop off at Gretna, quickly get married without telling anyone in advance, and carry on the journey to Cheshire. Part of the appeal of Gretna was its association with running off and tying the knot in secret, but we didn't do that in the end: it wouldn't have been fair on the rest of the family. Instead, we arranged for everyone to meet at Gretna. It made sense.

We almost missed our own big day, however, when we passed our witnesses on the motorway heading in the wrong direction. We were so confused by this that we too missed the turn-off for Gretna and had to carry on down the road to Carlisle, turn around and head north again. We made it – just.

There were about 20 people there to celebrate our big day, far more than we had expected, including Stuart and his fiancée, Amanda, as well as little Joshua in his buggy. Claire was there, too, as was my mum, who came with her sister-in-law, and my stepsister Jacqui and her grandson. A dear and loyal friend also came along, but waited outside the registry office with her partner and her mother. That was a great surprise and meant so much to me.

I had hoped that Dad would attend, because back in 1984, when I married Jim, my father being there was the one thing I dearly wanted. Now that I was in contact with him again, I thought he might make it second time around, but unfortunately his wife was poorly and he didn't manage. That was the only disappointment that day, however.

Malcolm and I walked into the registry office hand in hand, though when I look back at photographs today, it looks more like I am dragging him in to get married! I still hated being the centre of attention, even after having spent years in front of the TV cameras campaigning for a public inquiry, and I wanted the ceremony over and done with as quickly as possible. In many respects, it was more about getting the legal formalities over and done with, and getting back to the rest of our lives. It was the kind of wedding you could have had in your lunch hour, put it that way.

After the very quick ceremony was over and the photos had been taken, a number of us carried on down the M74 and M6 before stopping off at the first service station we came across. It became the impromptu venue for the wedding breakfast, with Burger King providing the meal of choice. It might not have been the most lavish or appropriate, but boy was it delicious.

Next stop on the road south was another service station, where we dropped off Malcolm's boys with his ex-wife so she could take them for a few days. When Ben and Stephen saw their mum, they ran towards her waving their button-holes and saying they had a flower for her. She smiled and thought it was a lovely gesture – at least she did until the boys said it was from their dad's wedding!

In the evening, we went to Ellesmere Port to stay with my brother James and sister-in-law Charlene and have a bit of a party. They had decked their house out with 'Just Married' banners and balloons, and there was champagne on ice. Dad, who likes to bake, had made two wedding cakes for us – one was a traditional Scottish fruit cake and the other was just a sponge for anyone not keen on fruit – and, considering his illness, he made a fabulous job of them.

Our first night of married life was spent on a double airbed on Charlene and James's floor but, nevertheless, we'd had a special day. It had been exactly as we had wanted it to be: just a basic, no frills, no fuss ceremony in front of the people who mattered most to us.

We didn't even have a honeymoon. Instead, the next morning Malcolm dropped me off at yet another service station on the M6, where I met Jim. I waved my new husband off, got into my ex-husband's car and drove away. We were off for the Army Board of Inquiry hearing into James's death.

As I sat in the passenger seat and watched the rain bouncing off the front bonnet, I wondered how many newly married women spend the first few days of married life with their ex-husbands. Not many, I am sure. It was a typical British summer's day: thunderous grey skies, heavy rain and humidity. But there was a tension in the air between us too. Jim and I had separated in May 2001 and had maintained an amicable relationship, but I knew today would be particularly difficult for him, as I was no longer just his ex-wife. As of 24 hours ago, I was now someone else's wife.

It wasn't an easy time for either of us. We had been forced together on this journey to the inquiry through no fault of our own. The excitement of the previous day still gave me butterflies, and I was very aware of the shiny new wedding ring gleaming on my finger, but part of me wanted to try to hide it from Jim so as to not make him feel like I was rubbing it in his face. By the same token, I was so proud and happy to be a new wife again.

There was no issue about leaving Malcolm behind less than 24 hours after our wedding, and he completely understood that James, and anything that would help me get to the bottom of his death, was still a priority in my life. It wasn't the first time it had happened – during the coroner's inquest in 2006 I was away from home for three weeks with my ex-husband – and it's unlikely to be the last either.

When I returned a couple of days later, after the Board

of Inquiry, I brought Jim back to Charlene's house with me, and he had dinner with us and even stayed over. There are not many men who would tolerate this kind of behaviour, especially just after tying the knot, but being accepting is one of the qualities I love about Malcolm. During the height of our campaigning, while Jim was being photographed by my side every other day, Malcolm was quietly in the background supporting me through it all and never once complained. He was by my side when I learned James was dead, he was there when I went to view his body, and he made sure I made it through the funeral. He was, and still is, my rock.

Malcolm is one of those rare people who always seems to be cool, calm and collected, and during the worst of what was thrown at me he was a steadying influence. The journalist Nicola Barry once even wrote that the words 'laid back' were probably invented just for him. It was so apt. Malcolm is one in a million, and I don't know if I could have coped with the past decade without him. If you ask me, he deserves a medal.

As I have already said, I first met Malcolm via the Internet, as it was becoming clearer by the day that my marriage to Jim was on the rocks. It was early in 2000 and message boards and chat rooms were becoming popular, so out of curiosity I went online to meet and interact with new people. However, it didn't take long to discover that many men on these forums were after one thing and one thing only, and I was quite offended by some of the sordid messages I was receiving.

Then there was Malcolm.

When I said I wasn't after a relationship, he said, 'Fine, so what else do you want to talk about?' We chatted about so many things in those first few exchanges, and we quickly hit it off.

I knew instinctively that this stranger cared for me, even

though we had never met face to face, and every time we chatted he made me feel special. I had suffered at the hands of so many people throughout my life that it was amazing to suddenly feel that I mattered to someone else.

I didn't feel as if I were cheating on my husband or anything, because by then Jim and I were leading separate lives, and the stress and tension in the house in Perth was becoming unbearable.

It's fair to say I was nervous that first time I eventually plucked up the courage to meet Malcolm in person, about a year after we had found one another online. To get down to Reading, I had to take an overnight coach from Perth to London and then catch a connecting bus. I was supposed to meet him in a car park at the back of a small shopping precinct, and he had sent me a picture of his car and told me to look out for it. When I got off the bus in Reading, I went into a cafe for a cup of tea and sat there thinking to myself, 'What on earth are you doing, Yvonne?' This mini-adventure to meet a strange man was so out of character for me, and anyone who knew me would never have believed I'd done it. It was as if I was having some kind of midlife crisis, and I almost got on the next bus and headed straight back to Scotland. Thank goodness I didn't.

Malcolm had sent me a photograph of himself, but when he finally pulled up in his car, I didn't recognise him at all: he was better-looking than the picture had suggested. His two boys were in the back of the car, so I jumped in the front and he leaned over and gave me a peck on the cheek. There was no awkwardness, as we felt we had known one another all our lives, but it did take me a while to overcome my anxiety. I was feeling guilty about leaving my children behind in Perth while I headed south. I had told James, Stuart and Claire only that I was going away for the weekend, not where or with whom.

When I eventually moved in with Malcolm on a permanent basis, a few months later, it was a huge risk because I had to give up my job in Perth, walk away from the family home and leave everything I had ever known for a man I'd befriended on the Internet. However, we had become very close, and the first signs of love were slowly starting to emerge. Malcolm made me happy, so in that respect it was an easy decision to make. James and Stuart were both also happy for me, and I had gone with their blessing, but leaving them behind will be one of the biggest regrets I will ever have. I decided to contribute financially to the household income in Perth so that the boys could continue to have some of the comforts they were used to, such as the satellite television, but it didn't make up for the fact that their mum wasn't there for them.

James took to Malcolm best of all, probably because he was the oldest and most mature of the children and could understand the difficulties I was having with his dad. They got on really well, and he even referred to Ben and Stephen as his brothers. Malcolm was as proud as anyone else when James passed out and became a real soldier. Stuart also got on well with Malcolm and did come to live with us for a short spell, but Claire was the least accepting of the new man in my life to begin with. That often led to fraught moments, given that she was the one who had initially decided to come down and stay with me in Reading. She was young and missed her dad terribly, and I can understand that. It was typical behaviour for a ten-year-old girl, and a decade on, I'm glad to say she and Malcolm now have a brilliant relationship.

My marriage to Malcolm is very different to the marriage I had with Jim. First time around I was young, and it was all about the adrenalin and excitement of the relationship, but with Malcolm I feel pure contentment. Perhaps that has just come with age and experience, but I do feel he is my soulmate. The love I feel for him is very deep, and it comes with a lot of admiration. Anyone able to tolerate what he has with me over the years has to be admired, and that makes me love him even more. He has always been there when I have needed him, he has taken a step back when he has needed to, and he has allowed Jim to stay in my life and have his rightful place as Claire, Stuart and James's dad. That says a lot about him.

That said, Malcolm doesn't have a single romantic bone in his body. He is simply not that way inclined. For instance, I can hint and hint that it would be nice to have some flowers, but instead of rushing down to the florist, he is more likely to give me £10 and tell me to go and buy some. So when he proposed via text message on the New Year's Eve of 2006, it was just typical Malcolm. I was actually at work helping some of my service users celebrate Hogmanay when he sent through the text, suggesting we make our relationship a bit more formal in the New Year and I become Mrs Heath. Romantic it was not, but it didn't matter, as I knew I wanted us to spend the rest of our lives together. Or, as Malcolm often put it, we planned to grow old together. We had been a couple for about five years and we had both felt for a while that marriage, and that kind of commitment, was the next logical step. It was only my campaigning and other aspects of our busy lives that had delayed it happening sooner.

I have to confess that after years of uncertainty and huge ups and downs, it's nice to be settled again and enjoying a stable family set-up. Malcolm and I now live with his two boys close to all my new extended family in Ellesmere Port. We moved there in 2011, on the day that Prince William married Kate Middleton, and as the nation rejoiced in the Royal Wedding, we were in a removal van somewhere on the M6. Ten years earlier I had gone to Reading to be with Malcolm when he needed me, then he and the boys later packed up and headed north to Scotland when I needed them there. Now I feel I need to be near the relatives I never knew I had until recently. It would have been folly for me to reunite with my dad, and discover I had brothers and sisters, then continue to live five hours' drive away. In addition, Dad wasn't in the best of health, while my brother James had also suffered a heart attack at a young age and had been diagnosed with multiple sclerosis. The one thing that my son's death has taught me is that you never know what tomorrow might bring, so I felt I had to be close to my family and be there to help whenever I could.

Malcolm was fine with the move, despite an element of it feeling like we were constantly moving the boys from pillar to post. He has always said that home is where the heart is, and his heart is with me. In any case, being in Ellesmere Port now means he is closer to his own parents in Reading, while his daughter, Alicia, has also moved here with us. My Claire is also now living around the corner from us with her fiance, Jamie, so we are surrounded by family.

We live in a three-bedroom mid-terrace house on the edge of town, and we couldn't be happier. Malcolm has been out of work for a long time now and is finding it frustrating. He did spend a short time as a landscape gardener last summer and enjoyed the outdoor nature of it, at least until the rain came down and the work dried up. I don't work, but Malcolm's youngest son Ben has autism, so I spend a lot of my time looking after him and making sure day-to-day life is a bit easier for him. The rest of the time I spend on myself, or visiting relatives, including Dad. In a reversal of roles, while I am now in England, my mum is back in Perth, and despite our earlier estrangement, I am in contact with her every day.

For the first time in 11 years, I feel content. I am at a

stage in my life where I have had to recognise that there are some things I will never be able to change, and I keep my strength only for what I can make a difference to. It has taken a decade to work that out, but I now know there is no point wasting time and effort battering my head against brick walls and trying to right wrongs I will never be able to fix. I will always continue to fight for James, but I also understand there will come a point at which there will be very little else I can do, and I will have to let go. That's hard, but I now realise that I have to enjoy life with the people I do still have with me. Life is so short.

It is tough being away from Stuart, Amanda and my grandchildren – Joshua now has two little brothers, Lewis and Thomas – in Perth, and it's also hard not being able to pop round to visit James's grave whenever I want to, but I try to get to Scotland as much as I can. I am thinking about going to the local council in Ellesmere Port to ask for a tree or some other kind of nice memorial I could have to commemorate James in a nearby cemetery, but I'm not sure how that would pan out. As for Malcolm and me: well, we will simply plod along and grow old together.

20. Never Forget

The Deepcut campaign had all but fizzled out by the turn of 2007. Having been floored by *The Deepcut Review*, there was little more we could do, and while we desperately hoped something would develop to allow us to start our crusade over again, nothing ever did. It was soul-destroying.

Jim and I had mustered enough energy to attend the Army Board of Inquiry into James's death in the summer of that year, but we knew it was hardly likely to throw up anything new and, being held by the Ministry of Defence, it certainly wasn't going to show Deepcut in a bad light. Initially we had been told we couldn't be there at all because it was deemed an internal Army affair, but the bureaucrats relented, presumably as a result of media pressure.

Held initially at an Army base in Marlborough, Wiltshire, for three days, with a two-day continuation in Perth at the Queen's Barracks, it was a fairly relaxed affair – far more relaxed than the coroner's inquest had been – and I was surprised at just how informal the proceedings were. Both Jim and I were also made to feel very welcome, which came as another pleasant surprise. As we watched, a number of witnesses were called in and questioned about the circumstances of James's death, or were asked general questions about what the Princess Royal Barracks was like to live and work in. What they said didn't paint a very good picture of the camp, but all that was common knowledge by now.

To be honest, we had heard almost all of the evidence before during the coroner's inquest, but I did feel I learned much more about Deepcut as an Army base during the time that James was stationed there. We also found out more about the day-to-day life James had had and what some of the senior officers had thought about him. His record showed that when he signed up, he was described as a bright prospect who had 'maturity beyond his age'. The recruitment officer had also noted that James was not affected by his parents' separation. That was a relief for me to hear, because for years the Army had kept trying to tell me James was immature and upset by life at home.

Prior to Privates Donnelly and McGrath giving their evidence – just as they had during the 2006 inquest – I had a long, hard think about how we could all move on from this point, and I pondered over how I felt about these two young men. There was no point in feeling anger or hatred towards them; I felt hatred was a very heavy burden to bear. During the inquest, I had watched them being put through hell, and I wondered how I would feel if they were my sons, and how the whole Deepcut experience would affect their futures. I decided that when they had finished their testimonies, I would reach across and shake their hands, and that's what I did. These two lads, whatever their involvement or lack of involvement in James's death, will have to live with that night for the rest of their days. They had suffered enough, and I needed to make my own peace with them and tell them I didn't hate them. Their sense of relief was palpable.

It was during the Board of Inquiry that we met Lieutenant Colonel Laden, the commanding officer of the barracks, for the first time. He offered no personal condolence; instead, under oath and in front of his fellow officers, he turned to me and Jim and said that we had ruined his life. Lt Col. Laden said that on the night James had died, he was attempting reconciliation with his wife and that had been interrupted because of the shooting. He moaned about the palaver, and having to arrive at the scene with all the blue lights of the emergency vehicles flashing, when all he really wanted to do was be with his wife. Lt Col. Laden also ranted about all the negative publicity surrounding Deepcut brought on by our campaigning, and insisted he took no blame for any of the deaths. His parting shot to us was, 'We will never be friends.'

Ruined his life? We had lost James on his watch, and our lives had been turned upside down by the death of a son. To me, his attitude, and his general sense of self-importance, simply typified the problem within the Army as a whole. This was the same man who had sent a very impersonal letter of supposed condolence when James died, the same man who had not come to the funeral when he was expected to, the same man who had sat directly behind us reading a newspaper and looking completely uninterested during the coroner's inquest. It was the Army's final insult to us, and to this day my blood boils thinking about that man. We have never heard from him, or of him, since that day, and I'm not even sure if he is still at Deepcut.

It took almost two full years for the Ministry of Defence to release the inquiry's findings, which recorded an open verdict, mirroring the 2006 inquest. As expected, the Armed Forces Minister, by this time Bob Ainsworth, immediately ruled out any possibility of a public inquiry on the back of the report. Five years earlier when Geoff Hoon had denied us an inquiry, it had felt like the end of the world; it was a scandal reported in all the newspapers and on television. This time around, in May 2009, the latest refusal only warranted a few paragraphs in the press, but we simply shrugged our shoulders and carried on. It was the same old story.

With Labour's defeat in the 2010 general election, we had hoped that we might finally win a public inquiry from the new coalition government. Certainly the majority of politicians who had been on our side from 2002 were either Liberal Democrats or Conservatives. The Lib Dems, in particular, had always been extremely supportive, and Nick Harvey, the man who took over as Armed Forces Minister, had previously wanted a public inquiry to be held. It wasn't to be. He might well have demanded answers of the Labour government when in opposition, but the moment he took up office himself, he suddenly washed his hands of us and of the campaign. On 13 June 2010, just weeks after the coalition was formed, he told the *Sunday Express*, 'After coming to the office of Armed Forces Minister it is clear to me that officials have looked into this issue in depth. There is no public or Service interest in pursuing a public inquiry.' Oh really?

We have now tried every political party without success. In the past eleven years, we have lobbied two governments, three prime ministers, three defence secretaries, three armed forces ministers, hundreds of MPs, the Army and the police. There is nowhere else to go in Britain. We have reached the end as far as pushing for a public inquiry through the UK parliament is concerned.

We know the Army hasn't exactly come out of the Deepcut affair smelling of roses: frankly, I will always be convinced that many aspects of the deaths were simply covered up. We know the police made a mess of the four investigations. We know the various reviews, inquests and inquiries over the years uncovered a shocking catalogue of bullying at Deepcut, and a climate of fear within the Army in general. But it is also now clear to us that no British government will ever hold a public inquiry:

officialdom is too fearful of the impact it would have on the reputation of the Army and how it would affect recruitment figures.

More than a decade on from the launch of the Deepcut campaign, none of the families are any closer to finding out what happened to our children in their last moments. The Princess Royal Barracks themselves will also soon be no more, after the government announced in 2008 that they were to be closed and sold off at some point between 2013 and 2016. We all have mixed emotions about that. Personally, while I wish I had never heard of the name Deepcut, I don't think it is right that it should simply disappear from existence. In a way, it feels like the place where James, Geoff, Cheryl and Sean died is going to be erased from history. I often go back to the barracks to be close to the spot where James spent the last few moments of his short life, but none of us will be able to do that soon if the site is transformed, as is planned, into a giant housing development with 1,200 new homes. The Royal Logistic Corps will move on to a new £300 million purpose-built site in Hampshire, and forget about its tarnished link with Deepcut.

We can never forget, however, and we haven't quite yet abandoned hope of finding out what happened to our loved ones. Indeed, we have decided to take it upon ourselves to turn detective and continue seeking out other avenues that might uncover the missing link. For example, Surrey Police has never published the full case notes relating to the investigation into the four deaths, and this is where we have started our work. The files – which contain everything from witness statements to the results of forensic tests and crime-scene photographs – have only ever been viewed in part by the coroner and by the Commons Defence Select Committee, but we now want access to all of them. We don't know what the case notes might hold, but we harbour hope that they can raise possible leads to explore. By its own admission, Surrey Police said officers had made a number of mistakes in investigating James's death, so perhaps we can capitalise on some of them and uncover a missing piece of the puzzle.

There is no reason for us not to have the files, yet various Freedom of Information requests have been refused on the grounds that the files are 'too large' and 'too costly' to be made public. What nonsense. Our legal team has been told it can look through some of the paperwork but on a read-only basis, and nothing can be photocopied. However, it will take the lawyers – who are not even being paid a fee to work on our behalf, and only undertake Deepcut business as a favour to us – a considerably long time to examine the files. Even then, their priority is to fee-paying clients, so we don't know when that might be, if at all.

So many potential leads were missed: we were told so by the police on numerous occasions. For instance, on the final day of the coroner's inquest it emerged that a chauffeur driving guests to the wedding taking place outside the Officers' Mess on the night James died was never questioned by detectives. He had been parked yards from where the shooting took place, and then left the barracks later in the evening, when all the commotion had died down. I know the driver was sent a questionnaire to fill in by the police – all the people at the wedding were – but even if he didn't think he'd seen anything, he might have. We need to find this man and speak with him properly. Likewise, I received an email from two of the wedding guests telling me they hadn't been questioned at the time either, and no door-to-door inquiries were carried out at the row of civilian houses directly opposite the perimeter fence where James's body was found.

Surrey Police didn't do its job properly, we know that now, so as far as I am concerned, it is never too late to go back over the investigations and look again with a fresh eye. In 2011, a damning final report by Devon and Cornwall Police into the Surrey force's handling of the Deepcut case made for interesting, and eye-opening, reading. At 140 pages long, it was a hefty document that found that the detectives who had promised us they would get to the bottom of the deaths were, from the outset, actually working under the assumption that they were self-inflicted. As a result, possible suspects were never spoken to. For instance, eyewitnesses spoke about rumours of an 'unknown white male' having killed Cheryl James, yet no attempts were made to identify this individual. How could this be? How could the police possibly have investigated the cases properly if the mindset from the very start was suicide? Colin Sutton, a retired detective chief inspector with Surrey Police, and the man who was the lead investigating officer into James's death, confessed to the BBC, 'The message I found I was getting from above was we need to conduct an investigation which is thorough and open, but at the same time there was another clear message: these were suicides weren't they, and that is where it is going to end up, and that is what you will end up proving.'

It was disgusting. When we were presented with the report during a meeting with Surrey Police, I got up and walked out. I was so angry I felt I could easily have walked up to the senior officers and punched them squarely in the face.

In his conclusion to *The Deepcut Review*, Nicholas Blake had hinted that there was more information available about the deaths of our loved ones than we have seen. Intriguingly, he wrote, '[The families are] in the unhappy position of not having seen the available material, to which this Review has had access, relating to their child's death . . . The families are, therefore, unable to form their own judgement as to whether the Review's conclusions are the appropriate

239

ones.' He's right. We all know there is other information out there – the Surrey Police file for a start – and we have to get access to it.

I am also keen to see if there might be any link between James's death and that of another Royal Logistic Corps soldier in Germany just a month later. As I have mentioned before, Private David Shipley, 20, was found drowned in a paddling pool containing only 12 inches of water. He had been posted to Bielefeld soon after the shooting, along with the last recruits who saw James alive. What intrigues me most is that he had been with James at Deepcut and had actually reported for the same guard duty that night, but was stood down and not required. The coroner's inquest into Private Shipley's death recorded an open verdict, with the coroner stating that he did not believe the evidence of soldiers who claimed the young recruit, from Barrow, had been thrown in the pool during 'gentlemanly horseplay'. The coroner said he had 'suspicions' about what went on, while *The Deepcut Review* also mentioned that the police who investigated Shipley's death similarly found his fellow soldiers somewhat obstructive when questioned. Perhaps some of them would be willing to talk now about both deaths? More than a decade has passed since my son died, and my feeling is that there are people out there who do know something, but were afraid to come forward in 2002 and might readily speak out today.

There are so many questions about James's death that remain unanswered; there are so many ifs and maybes. I can't help but think back to the chat I had with him on the phone a few days before he died, when he asked me for £100. He said at the time it was for a trip to Spain with the squadron, telling me that he needed the extra cash to be able to enjoy the nights out. Yet we learned that the Royal Logistic Corps never had any trip to Spain lined up and James had lied to us. Why, we just do not know. We knew he had financial worries: perhaps he owed someone money and that played a part in his death.

I'm also curious about what it was James had to tell his girlfriend as he boarded the minibus on that fateful night. From what we heard from her evidence at the coroner's inquest, he seemed quite eager to tell her something, but never got the chance. What was it? Might it have been about a problem? Similarly, I ask myself all the 'what ifs': what if James hadn't have been on guard duty that night; what if he hadn't been given the gun by Private Donnelly; what if he hadn't gone for a smoke? Would he still be alive today? I suppose there's no point in speculating, because it won't bring James back, but you've got to wonder.

We do have another option tucked up our sleeves in our search for the truth: our lawyers have told us that we can take our demand for a public inquiry to the European Court of Human Rights in Strasbourg. However, before we decide to go down that route, we need to have some hard evidence that our loved ones did not kill themselves. In many respects, that is probably the most important reason for gaining access to the police files, and we are confident we will eventually get to read every single document relating to the investigation. Europe would be our last throw of the dice as far as a public inquiry is concerned, but I'm not convinced we will ever get around to taking it forward on human rights grounds. In any case, if after reading the police documents there is still nothing to suggest foul play or an accident with the four deaths then we might have to accept what everyone has been telling us for ten years: they all took their own lives.

To be honest, I have never fully been against the theory that James did kill himself. As I've said before, in many ways I would prefer that, because it would mean he had control over his own destiny in his final moments. I just want the truth, and if that truth is that my James shot himself in the head – and someone brought forward that missing piece of evidence to show that is exactly what he did – then fine. If another soldier came forward and was to tell me, 'Mrs Heath, I was there, I saw him do it. I tried to stop him, but I couldn't. I'm sorry,' then my ordeal would be over. However, neither can I truly accept that conclusion without some proof.

At the very beginning of the campaign, I did believe James was murdered, but now I am not so sure. Throughout the course of all the investigations and inquiries over the space of the past eleven years, there has never been one shred of credible evidence that he was an unpopular or disliked lad. In other words, there was no reason for anyone to kill him. Having said that, no one knows what went on in the last seven hours of his life and what may, or may not, have happened.

Knowing what I do now about the barracks and the Army regime in general, I tend to think he probably died as a result of some prank that went wrong or during some kind of juvenile initiation ceremony. These were young, unsupervised soldiers out on guard duty with guns, and the opportunity was there for high jinks – and for a tragedy to occur. What I have not wavered on is my belief that James would not have wanted to take his own life.

Regardless of how he died, I truly believe there is someone out there that knows the truth but has not come forward for whatever reason. The parents of Cheryl James and Geoff Gray feel the same about their own children, just as they did back in 2002. Geoff and Diane have always insisted their son was murdered, and they will believe that until their dying days.

However, I'm not too sure how committed to the cause the other families will be the longer time passes. Certainly the Deepcut Four aren't as close as we once were. I can't remember the last time I heard from the Bentons, and it's only every other month now that I get a phone call or an email from Des James. As for Geoff and Diane, the couple that at one point in time we saw on a weekly basis, we have also drifted apart over the past five years or so, and our relationship is nowhere near what it once was. Daily chats became weekly, then fortnightly, then every so often. Now it's just the occasional note on Facebook or the odd email back and forwards. It's sad, in a way, and isn't the fault of anyone in particular; it is simply down to the fact that our campaign for a public inquiry ran out of steam. However, we all know that we are still there for one another whenever the need arises, and we'll have that special relationship for the rest of our days, even if it is from afar. The unique, if tragic, bond we share over the deaths of our children at Deepcut will never be lost.

I used the tenth anniversary of James's death in March 2012 to try to rekindle some interest in Deepcut, and I will continue to do so until the day I die. After so long, and particularly with so little happening, there is a danger that the public will simply forget. That scares me. Deepcut is a story with no end, and it should never be viewed as just a minor blot on the British Army without a proper conclusion as far as the four deaths is concerned. However you look at it, it was one of the most shameful episodes in the history of Britain's Armed Forces.

People often say that time heals, but I'm not so sure. Yes, eventually we will be able to get on with the rest of our lives; yes, one day we might finally be provided with the missing answers. By the end of 2016, even the barracks will be long gone, having been reduced to rubble. But the pain of losing a child: that will stay with me for ever. Deepcut will never go away.

Afterword

I often imagine what James would be like today if he was still alive. He would be 28 years old now, but in my mind I can only see him as the teenager I waved goodbye to as he drove off in the car, smiling and with that cheeky glint in his eye. If only we knew then what the future had in store for us. My son had his whole life ahead of him that night, but it was all taken away with one single bullet. But what if James hadn't gone to work that March afternoon; what if he hadn't swapped the guard duty and instead stayed in Reading with me for that one extra day? Would it have made a difference? Would he be alive and well today, and be married with children, like his little brother? Would he even still be in the Army? Perhaps he might be serving in Afghanistan and be regarded as a hero, like so many of our other soldiers. We will never know.

Some of James's school friends still keep in touch with me, and I enjoy seeing them and hearing about what they are doing in their own lives. At the same time, I feel a little twinge of sadness inside because I know my boy should be doing the same and enjoying his life to the full. As I've said before, I still look for James when I see groups of youngsters, only to have to remind myself he's not going to be there: he's dead. It hurts all over again.

One of the most difficult days was Stuart's wedding in July 2009. I tried so hard to be happy – I wanted to feel happy and be there for Stuart and Amanda – but it was impossible. I smiled for the cameras and laughed at the jokes during the speeches, but inside I was broken. James should have been there by his brother's side. He should have been the one who organised the stag do, he should have been the one who kept the rings safe and told the embarrassing stories of Stuart's childhood when the time came. Instead, one of Stuart's friends was his best man, and even he acknowledged that he was only filling the void and standing in for the man who couldn't make it. 'James would have been so proud of you today, Stuart,' he said as we raised a toast to him and shed a few tears. We carried on with the rest of the day, but James was never far from my mind.

I now have three lovely grandsons by Stuart. Obviously they never had the opportunity to meet their Uncle James, but they do speak about him as if they know him, and they enjoy tending to his 'garden' in Perth. James would have loved them and no doubt would have spent too much time teaching them about all sorts of mischief from his own childhood. My oldest grandson Joshua has James as his middle name as a tribute to his late uncle, and it's lovely to think his name carries on through his nephew.

In 2007, a street in Perth was also named after James, and I am sure he would have been tickled pink about that. He might even find it amusing: a street named after him. Collinson View leads off from the main road in Perth at a set of traffic lights, meaning that drivers who stop there will see the name. It was an idea that came about from a local councillor called Gordon Hunter, who wanted to create a mark of honour for James, and for me and Jim for all the campaigning we had done to raise awareness of the Deepcut issue. We'd done Perth proud, he said. I was so touched and was very emotional. Even now when I go back to Perth and walk past Collinson View, I feel very proud.

The loss of a child is, by far, the worst thing that can happen to any parent. I liken the pain of being without James to how it would feel to lose a limb: part of me is missing and I miss it badly, and I feel the constant pain of it not being there, but I must learn to adapt so I can get through every day without crumbling.

I don't suppose I will ever quite believe James has gone: it hurts too much to face that reality. People have said I should 'come to terms with it' or 'move on', but I don't think it's that easy. I don't think it's possible at all. Part of me died when James died. I am no longer the same person as I was in 2002. I can't enjoy things the same way I used to, and I feel I can't love in the same way I used to either for fear of being hurt again. In many ways, my body and my emotions have been numbed by what has happened to me.

The past 11 years have completely changed me as a person and have also altered my views on fairness and justice. I was never very good at dealing with confrontation and always believed in treating others as you would wish to be treated yourself. Oh boy, was I naive to expect those same values from others in positions of power, particularly within the police and the Army. Indeed, it's fair to say I have had my eyes well and truly opened about how much petty politics influence both institutions on a day-to-day basis.

My children were brought up to trust and respect a policeman, and to seek one out if ever they were in any kind of trouble. It was something I believed in myself, having had it instilled in me when I was young. But when you have been let down, as I have been, by those very same people then you have to ask yourself if that trust was misguided. I've pondered this so many times over the past decade, and the answer is always the same: yes, it was. What reason would I have had to ever suspect that the police would not treat my son's death as suspicious? Or that they wouldn't even bother to investigate until the media had forced their hand? Why, too, was it left to me to phone around all the police stations in Surrey to ask if anyone was even looking into the shooting? And what about the indignity of having to be forced into exhuming my own son's body because the police had made a mess of the original post-mortem? I should never have had to do that, and I hope it never happens to anyone else in a similar situation. Don't forget that it latterly emerged that detectives had been instructed from above to prove all the Deepcut deaths were suicides rather than attempt to solve them. No, trust and respect are no longer things I have for the police in this country. You can't blame me, either.

As I said at the beginning of the book, if you took me back 12 years and told me my life would pan out the way it has, I don't think I would believe you. It has been an extraordinary journey, and my world has been turned completely upside down. Jim and I have met people, and been to places and done things we never envisaged we would do in our lifetimes. Prior to 2002, for instance, I had only ever been to London once, on a sightseeing tour bus. By the end of 2003, Jim and I had been up and down from Perth almost 40 times and were on first-name terms with staff on the train, and were sometimes given free upgrades to first class. Before 2002, I had never met a MP and, if I'm honest, I don't think I even knew who the local one was for us in Perth. Since then we've been to the House of Commons countless times, met hundreds of politicians, confronted ministers, and even joined some of the friendlier MPs in the Westminster bar. We've also taken part in several documentaries and innumerable news broadcasts, joined the likes of Penny Smith and John Stapleton on the famous *GMTV* sofa, had two plays written about our experiences, and had a dressing room of our own to appear on *Richard & Judy*. In our home town we have become well-kent faces and are still stopped in the street by strangers and asked how we are, or given a pat on the back and told 'keep up the good work'.

It has been surreal, to say the least, but all of it was done without a second thought. It was simply a means to an end, a way of getting answers. The whole process has been a roller coaster of emotions, with our hopes of winning a public inquiry being built up time and time again, only to be let down with an almighty thud by the government.

There is no reason not to hold a public inquiry into Deepcut, and I will never understand why every single political party in office has ruled it out. In 2010, the coalition announced that, following years of pressure from campaign groups, it would allow a public inquiry into the 1994 Chinook crash that killed 29 people on the Mull of Kintyre. In other words, there is precedent for examining historic cases. So why not Deepcut? I still wonder what it is ministers are afraid of. Surely it can't just be that they fear Army recruitment figures flatlining. If it is, then that is a scandal in itself: the government has done more to decimate the number of people serving in the Armed Forces through cutbacks than anything a Deepcut public inquiry would ever do. Indeed, in January 2013 the Ministry of Defence announced that 5,300 troops and 50 senior officers are to be made redundant, in the biggest tranche of cuts since the 1990s. This is in addition to the 2,800 axed in September 2011 and 3,700 in June 2012.

In the aftermath of the publication of the official report into the 1989 Hillsborough tragedy in September 2012, our barrister John Cooper QC wrote a poignant article in *The Independent* in which he said that 'a great many injustices have certainly gone on in the past that have yet to be exposed'. He continued, 'There are people from all walks of life who know, just as the Hillsborough campaigners knew, that great wrongs have been perpetrated. The deaths at Deepcut are just one example; the families of four young people who died at the barracks are still treated by government and the police as borderline crackpots.' He's right there.

Deepcut is a name I wish I had never heard of. Not only did it take my son's life, it took a part of me too. I have spent so many years consumed by it, to the point that I almost jeopardised the relationships I have with my surviving children. Indeed, sometimes I feel as if I could happily drive the bulldozer through the camp myself when the time comes for it to be demolished.

That said, I believe we have made some differences to life within the Princess Royal Barracks and within the Army in general. Many experts even say that Deepcut is now one of the safest barracks in Britain as a result of all the attention it has had. For example, young trainees no longer do routine guard duty without supervision; this role is now undertaken by more mature and experienced soldiers. New recruits and their families are now given information booklets when the trainees move to the camp, explaining more about the garrison and providing all the necessary contact numbers for relatives to use if they have any concerns. Changes have been made in the ratio of instructors to recruits, and there are stricter policies for the handling of firearms. What's more, when it comes to untimely deaths the military and civilian police are both now clear about who has primacy, meaning that a proper investigation can begin from the outset.

The other thing we have achieved through our

campaigning is that we have made the public more aware of what Army life is like, and raised concerns about the way in which recruits can be treated. No one wants young soldiers wrapped up in cotton wool and served breakfast in bed every day, but neither should they be bullied, beaten or placed in any undue danger by the actions of over-zealous officers. It is not too much to ask, surely. We realise that the men and women serving our country might sadly lose their lives in action, but we don't expect them to be put in harm's way in the relative safety of the Army training camp by their own peers.

None of the changes we have helped force through have brought me any closer to finding out what happened to James on 23 March 2002. We didn't campaign to make the Army safer, or to bring about change in the standards of care within the Armed Forces. They became accidental, but welcome, coincidences. The only thing I set out to do was get justice for my son, but I haven't succeeded. Not yet anyway. I will always hold on to the hope that one day someone who saw or heard something will come forward and speak out.

The Army had a duty of care to James. When we signed his parental consent form, they took on the role of *in loco parentis*, but they failed in the extreme. Interestingly, that role has now been removed from the Army for recruits under the age of 18. During the Board of Inquiry, Lt Col. Laden said he had repeatedly flagged up his concerns regarding the lack of permanent supervisory staff at Deepcut, but was always told by his superiors to make the most of the staff he had at his disposal, however inadequate. Some of those staff, we learned, had to work 72-hour weeks and were toiling through sheer exhaustion. How could they possibly be expected to do their jobs properly and maintain a disciplined and effective Army training camp? They had an impossible task. Had the top brass listened to Laden's concerns at the time, I believe James would still be alive today, and to that end I hold them responsible for his death.

Nothing will ever bring James back, but at least if we got a public inquiry, we could honestly say we have done everything we can for Sean, Cheryl, Geoff and James, and allow them to rest in peace.

When I look back on my life, it would be easy to feel sorry for myself, but I refuse. I tend not to dwell too much on what has happened to me over the years, from the playground bullies to the abusive uncle and the death of James. It would be too difficult. In any case, there will always be someone who has suffered worse than I have and is perhaps still suffering, in silence. I don't like sympathy either, and find it unwelcome; it only serves to weaken me. Indeed, I believe that each blow I am dealt is given to me for a reason, and you could argue that surviving my horrific childhood made me strong enough to deal with the loss of my son, and go on to fight for justice for him. What I do know is that losing James has made me a stronger, more determined person.

Deepcut is now in a little box on the shelf, which I choose to open or not. Having said that, I still have days when I don't want to get out of bed and face another day, of course I do. It's particularly difficult on dates with special significance, such as James's birthday, or the passing of yet another anniversary of his death. I agonise over how I should mark these days: they aren't for celebrating, but neither can they be ignored, and it's hard knowing what to do.

Whatever terrible things have gone on in my life, whatever pain and hurt so many people have caused me over the years, nothing will ever compare to what I felt the moment I learned my son was gone. Losing my James was, by far, the deepest cut of all. However, I have somehow managed to find the strength to carry on, even if all I do at times is go through the motions of day-to-day life. Somewhere in my heart I know I will see James again, and that the void he left will be filled once more. One day I will hold him close again and give him that cuddle that never was, and when I do, I'll be able to tell him not to worry any more, that everything is fine, his mum is here. For ever.

Acknowledgements

ᐯᐱ

It was a difficult decision to write a book about James's death, and it involved a great deal of soul-searching and delving into parts of my past I had tried to forget a long time ago. At times, it has been hard reliving some of the events, while at others it has been of great therapeutic value and reminded me of the happier moments when Jim and I enjoyed life with our three children.

Indeed, there are many people without whom I wouldn't have had the courage or strength to put pen to paper. My son, Stuart, and daughter, Claire, are the reason I do still get up every morning: they give me the will to live. My three grandsons, Joshua, Lewis and Thomas, are the lights of my life, and they give me reason to smile again. Then there is my dear, dear husband, Malcolm, who has been my rock. He has put up with so much over the years, including being called Mr Collinson on numerous occasions. However, he never falters, he is always there for me, and I don't know where I would be without him.

The families of Sean, Cheryl and Geoff were in my thoughts constantly as I put this book together, and I hope they find reading it as helpful to them as it was to me writing it. We have all been through so much together in the most tragic of circumstances. Though the Deepcut Four was a group I never wanted to belong to, I could not have wished for better people to be part of it with me. We all continue to live with the hurt and the agony on a daily basis. In many ways, the Bentons have perhaps suffered the most. Harry Benton died in the summer of 2011 without truly knowing what happened to his son. Then, shortly before Christmas 2012, Sean's brother Lee died at the age of 29. How Linda copes I'll never know.

The support we have had from so many people as we fought the Deepcut campaign was overwhelming, and I will be eternally grateful to the politicians, charity groups and ordinary members of the public who tried so hard to help us secure a public inquiry. It is a tragedy we cannot have the ending we all desire.

Last, but not at all least, I must thank my co-writer Derek Lambie, who has been an invaluable support over the years, both in his former role at the *Scottish Sunday Express* and also now with this book.

A massive thank you to each and every one of you. Let us never forget the names of Sean Benton, Cheryl James, Geoff Gray and James Collinson.

Yvonne Collinson Heath, March 2013